THE POWER
OF THE PACK

THE POWER OF THE PACK

The Adventures and Misadventures of a Dog Trainer

PIERCE H. RUSSELL JR.

The Power of the Pack:
The Adventures and Misadventures of a Dog Trainer

ISBN: 979-8-9882998-6-8

Cover design by Kelsey Harding

Cover photograph by Lana Carson

Author photograph by Pierce H. Russell Jr.

Spine pawprint by Sasha Olivero for the Noun Project

Some names have been changed for privacy.

For Lana
and all the dogs who loved me

CONTENTS

PART I

PART II

PART III

Part I

PIERCE H RUSSELL JR

BEAR SETS THE HOOK

Upon being deployed by the US Army to Camp Ames, South Korea in the early 1970s, I was assigned to the motor pool to keep their books. Not sure what to expect, I walked into a den of thieving mechanics. They misappropriated inventory and bullied me to cover their "enterprise." It was like the antics Sergeant Bilko faced on *The Phil Silvers Show*—but without the humor. Chafing at the intimidation, I was miserable there.

So I was in luck when my friends who were sentry dog trainers told me that the latest handler partnered with a dog named Bear had been reassigned because he couldn't control the canine's ninety pounds of muscled weapon. I volunteered to fill the handler position, and with a few good words put in by my buddies, the officer in charge of the Military Police (MP) dog platoon gave me the chance to escape the thugs at the motor pool. I said "hasta la vista" to creative accounting.

Now I had to prove myself. Did I mention I'd never met Bear?

When the day came, the platoon sergeant handed me a leash. We walked down the kennel's concrete corridor centered between outside runs of chain-link fencing— ten six-by-five-foot enclosures per side, each with a raised doghouse.

At Bear's run, I was instructed to lift the latch, enter with confidence, and resecure the latch immediately. Then I was to leash the dog, exit the pen, and follow the sergeant to the fenced training area for some basic obedience and obstacle work.

"Show no fear," he cautioned.

Right.

Until that moment, I'd been so thrilled to escape the motor pool that I hadn't thought to be afraid. But Bear wasn't just *any* dog—he was a sentry dog, a powerful tool bred to work for the US Army and trained to detect, intimidate, and neutralize the enemy.

Was I scared? Roger that.

Did I have second thoughts? Nope. I wanted to face my fears. Bring it on.

Combining a deep breath with a short prayer, I moved in fast, fixed the latch behind me, and spun around. A blur filled my vision. The beast pinned me against the gate with his paws on my shoulders. Did I mention I was over six feet tall?

Inches away from my face and looking me straight in the eye was a magnificent Belgian Malinois-German shepherd mix. Black with a white chest, he had white slashes under his golden-brown eyes.

Bear

I tightened the muscles of my bladder and sphincter.

"Good boy, good boy, Bear," gurgled out of my mouth.

He licked my face.

Flooded with relief, I hooked the leash to his leather collar and stroked his hard flanks. I issued my first command, "Sit."

He sat.

Seizing the moment, I turned back to the gate, opened the latch, and marched Bear at a heel out to the training field. Adrenaline pulsed through my veins as we trained. Bear responded to my commands like we'd worked together for years. His reactions to me were both a surprise and delight, but I didn't have time to dwell on it. I just wanted to keep our dynamic going. My confidence rose, my fears lessened, and we settled into a groove.

Then revelation struck, clear as the blue sky above me: This was what I was put on earth to do.

The sergeant—satisfied that I had taken charge over the alpha-male attack dog—suggested I get some sleep for the following day's platoon initiation. Our session over, I returned Bear to his run and promised him I would be back.

I arrived the next morning ready for another challenge. Platoon mates dressed me in a thick padded suit resistant to the pressure of powerful bites. The collar came up to my chin, protecting my throat. I looked like the Michelin Man™. A few parts of the suit —the armpits and crotch—had thinner fabric flexible enough for limited movement. I wanted very much to avoid getting bitten in those areas.

I inquired about a helmet. They chuckled, and with no warning tipped me over. I toppled to the ground like a felled tree.

"Get up," barked the sergeant.

It was impossible.

"First lesson," he bellowed. "Stay on your feet at all times!"

Setting me upright, they briefed me on the process. A handler would enter the training field with his dog and drop its leash. Then he and the dog would approach me. I was to make noise, wave my arms, and "feed" one of my padded arms to the canine. They assured me that all sentry dogs went for the nearest moving body part. Once the dog latched onto me, I was to keep moving until the handler told me to freeze. I would get that command after the handler had retrieved the leash and restrained his dog.

The dogs practiced this daily. They lived for the bite especially when the "agitator," "meat," or "perp" froze because it signified a win.

When the first dog charged through the gate onto the field, its handler racing alongside at breakneck speed, I sure *felt* like meat. Dropping the lead, the handler commanded, "Get him."

The furry bullet covered the one hundred feet between us like a precision heat-seeking missile. I put my genetics and cultural roots to good use, roaring in brash New Yorker fashion while bouncing around on stiff legs and waving my arms. The canine torpedo hit my left arm with a savage, jaw-clamping chomp. I felt it all the way down to my toes despite being clad in durable combat boots. The snarling devil could shred anything I was wearing in minutes, if not seconds.

Shaking my arm with the attached brute, I rattled him around and hollered until the handler yelled, "Freeze."

I stood still.

When the handler then commanded, "Out. Watch him," the dog released my arm and lay down six feet away, eyes focused on me, ears up and fixed forward.

The soldier advanced and simulated a search, running his arms up and down my left side and then my right side. His canine partner observed my every motion, ready and willing to strike like a coiled snake. As I randomly pretended to hit his handler with my padded arms, the dog sprang at me immediately, fierce to protect its master.

Sentry dog (foreground) riveted on a "perp" in a padded suit

The thrill was exhilarating. My heart pounded, my hair stood on end, and my twenty-one-year-old body—brimming with adrenaline and testosterone—quivered like a taut bowstring. I loved the rush of that initiation.

After that first test of the day, I'd assumed I would be put through the routine again by a few more members of the platoon and their dogs. Turns out they had different plans: *All* of the handler-dog pairs had a go at me. I was unaware of how many teams comprised the platoon but soon found out. One after another, nineteen more handlers with maniacal grins released nineteen more foaming, barking, gnashing-mouthed furies at me. On their way from the gate to the fray, some handlers sauntered, some trotted, and some ran full-out.

Some dogs feinted at my arms but bit my padded thighs. Others shook me with supernatural force. I managed to improve in strength and nuanced skills. I learned that upon the Out command, some dogs let go right away while others had to be forced out of their hold. When a dog refused to release me, the handler straddled the dog, walked up the leash, then squeezed the dog's carotid artery while saying Out until it dropped its hold on me and came out of its trance.

When the whole platoon had finished, I unlaced and shed my cumbersome suit. Exhausted and soaked with sweat, I felt pounds lighter but was filled with a self-assurance I'd never experienced before. After dinner and some brews with my new handler mates, I slept like a baby. As I dressed the next morning, I noticed some bruises but no puncture wounds. Though my arms and legs ached like I had the flu, my spirit soared, gratified to know there was a place on this earth where I mattered and belonged.

I worked diligently with Bear, gaining ability and control. Because he was dog-aggressive, he would attempt to attack the other male dogs, which could result in costly wounds if he connected. I had to watch him like a hawk and keep him on a short leash during group training sessions.

If he lunged at a dog, I would yell "No" while employing a helicopter spin technique, pulling his leash one way then the other, and using his momentum to whirl him once around with all four paws in the air. He hated that loss of contact with the ground. As I corrected him, Bear eventually associated my "No" with the unwelcome spinning. In due course, the verbal command alone sufficed to stop his strikes.

The author on the right, straddling Bear

Camp Ames was a depot for nuclear warheads stored in concrete tunnels—we called them "herds"—built into the mountainsides. The installation was surrounded by two fences with barbed wire strung on top that traversed the heights of nearby mountains and the valley between them.

Watch towers (one at left) stood strategically along the wire. Tower duty on these small structures with no creature comforts could be hellish.

MP watch towers along the inner and outer barbed wire perimeters, Camp Ames, South Korea

Soldiers known as "tower rats" or "tower jockeys" of the 110th MP Company had to endure monotonous hours staring at densely vegetated terrain interspersed with scrubby bushland. Some succumbed to the dreary task and attempted suicide; sadly, some succeeded.

11

Every night, Bear and I walked a post on the strip between the inner and outer perimeters. The trees didn't bother me—I was accustomed to the forests of Vermont and upstate New York. Though we moved on roads bordered by six-foot-high walls of foliage that blocked my view, my four-legged partner had a super nose for scents. If he detected anyone within five hundred yards (depending on wind direction) beyond the outer wire, he would silently freeze in a point position to alert me.

There was a rub. During the summer, the scents and sounds of prowling leopard cats—small wildcats native to Asia—distracted Bear, who would persistently pull toward the outer ring of wire and nose around. Any dog tangling with one of these tough, compact cats could be torn to shreds by their sharp teeth and claws.

Sergeants warned us that if we were attacked by a rabid wildcat, we should empty our .45-caliber pistols at it and pray. I had barely qualified with the pistol—couldn't hit the side of a billboard over fifty yards away—but Bear didn't know that. Luckily, I never saw any of the cats materialize out of the thick undergrowth.

As my love for this amazing shepherd grew, our mutual trust and respect developed into an unbreakable bond, the strongest with any living creature I'd encountered yet in my life. When he was sick with worms, I nursed him day and night, cleaning him and his kennel run.

But despite our deepening connection, I was frustrated with Bear's performance on the obstacle course. The training was conducted semi-off-leash which meant that sometimes I would be holding his leash and other times I'd drop it for certain obstacles.

At the start of the course, Bear leapt over a hurdle into a half culvert about ten feet long. I dropped his lead and issued the crawl command. He sank down on his belly and wriggled low across the sand like a snake slithering away from a wildfire.

Once he was through that section, I raced next to him to grab the trailing leash before he came to the next obstacle, a free-standing window frame. But he emerged from the ditch like a shot from a cannon, and I failed to get ahold of his lead. He rocketed through the window. Going too fast to handle the balance beam that followed, Bear either jumped right over the beam or zipped along it smack into an inclined ladder just beyond.

We practiced over and over with little progress. I simply couldn't get him to slow down and apply some finesse to the balance beam. Another epiphany hit me: I was the problem. Running next to him along the course wasn't working, for him or for me.

So the next day when we stepped out onto the course, I took Bear entirely off-leash and said Free. Under a hot sun, from start to finish, he performed without me, unrestricted, and came to a sit position on the elevated platform that marked the end of the course.

No mistakes. Not one. He had controlled his speed.

I praised him with loving strokes and all the "good boys" I wished I'd had—but never received—from my mother and father.

The crux of this is that the first dog I trained was a dominant alpha sentry dog over which I had to be firmly and demonstrably dominant. With Bear by my side, I had confronted my fears. As I mastered control, I found that I could ease up on some things. When I paid better attention to how Bear and I interacted, I became a better trainer, learning to listen, watch, and reward good behavior when it happened. This is how I've worked with dogs over the course of my life ever since.

When it was time to go back to the US after my tour was up, I thanked Bear for everything he did for me and wished him well. I told him I would always carry his love in my heart, and I have. I'll never forget that incredible dog and the priceless gift he gave me—Bear transformed my outlook on life by revealing to me what I was meant to do.

BEGINNINGS

From birth until gravity got a firm grip on my middle-aged body, I rode an emotional rollercoaster between infinite highs and abysmal lows. Constant criticism and reminders of past faux pas played over and over in my head. To this mental distress add attention deficit hyper-activity disorder (ADHD), and the phrase "a piece of work" might come to mind. It's unpleasant to revisit certain periods of my life because doing so can overwhelm me with sadness. But sometimes you must acknowledge your truths before moving on.

It all began when my father Bud entered the Troy Savings Bank in Troy, New York, and was smitten with a brown-eyed, dark-haired teller. He was strapping handsome, and Leanore was a beauty with an affable nature. They fell in love and married in late 1940. Four years later my sister Linda came along, born while Bud was serving overseas in the US Army during World War II. He did not meet his first child until she was a little over one year old.

I was added to the family a few years after that, whelped on a June day in 1948. When the doc slapped my rear end, I like to think I beamed and let loose with a bellowing laugh. Born blond and blue-eyed like my dad, I looked the part of a Russell man. After I came home from the hospital, I began soaking up everything like a sponge, as babies and children do.

Beginning life exuberant and happy-go-lucky, as a boy I delighted in movement, and I loved playing and being outside. I wasn't diagnosed with ADHD until I was older and on my own—such a diagnosis didn't enter the mainstream until the 1980s. Unfortunately, kids in the 1950s and 1960s (and later) who couldn't pay attention were considered by many to be morally defective.

Growing up I heard loud arguments between my mother and father. We lived in a den of dysfunction, but at the time I didn't know that—I was only a kid. We ate breakfasts and dinners together in the kitchen. My parents fought like cats and dogs at many meals, flinging criticism, demands, sarcasm, and rancor back and forth across the table.

As an adult, I've since thought about what happened to their romance. Relationships swing from a high of infatuation and attraction to a low after falling back to earth when reality settles in. For my parents, the reality was harsh. Once the wooing ceased and the honeymoon ended, the interaction of their respective backgrounds and temperaments conspired to defeat them.

Leanore ("Sis" to her family, and "Sis" or "Lee" to friends) was tenacious and spunky. She and her older brothers were raised on a Speigletown property with enough land for extensive gardening. During the Great Depression, her working-class family not only grew potatoes and vegetables, but also raised chickens. Lee rung their necks and plucked them. Except for the fowl, she stood up for underdogs with considerable nerve.

Lee had started college in Erie, Pennsylvania, with plans to be a nurse but dropped out after her father died of a heart attack in 1938. Her hopes and dreams dissipated like fog driven off by a burning sun.

In contrast, my dad was a golden boy, the middle child of three—the only son from a well-to-do family. Bud graduated from an exclusive prep school and then college. Expected to follow in the footsteps of his father—a lawyer who moved on to a judgeship and was forever after referred to as The Judge—Dad then attended and graduated from Albany Law School. He at times used the extensive vocabulary he'd assimilated during his education to belittle and subjugate my mom.

The Judge, considered a pillar of society, had been involved in the founding of a local country club with other well-off patrons. Though Bud's ties to this country club existence appealed to my mother as the promise and thrill of a privileged life, inwardly she didn't always feel at ease with the milieu. She felt ill-matched and insecure in comparison to Bud's background. When Bud's attention to Lee switched from complimentary to disparaging, her Cinderella story lost its fairy-tale luster.

Intelligent and articulate in public, Bud managed (in part) to suppress his temper at his law office. His reservoir of ire filled up during the day. He had a short fuse at home where he laid down his own law and required perfection. Today he might be diagnosed with obsessive-compulsive disorder (OCD) and depression or bipolar disorder. My sister and I were raised in fear under the thumb of a control freak. We tiptoed around so as not to wake the beast.

I would sit at the kitchen table cowed by fear, as still as a child with ADHD could be. As I watched my dad—in my mind a massive predator—I'd freeze like prey attempting to disappear into the background. I would look for tells—signs to forewarn me of when he would lash out. I learned to keep my head down or leave the room when his face flushed and darkened because then he was a powder keg about to blow. He'd snap and corner my mom or me, hurling invectives or swiping at us with the meaty paw of a grizzly bear.

When he came home late from work, Lee took offense. He would enter the house with his tie still knotted at the collar of his white dress shirt (ironed "lovingly" with spray starch)—the knot taut like the anger he held within. Exchanging his suit coat for a cardigan, he'd put the coat in his closet where it hung limp from his withering vexation at the office. He needed to unwind in peace and quiet, but Mom would pounce on him with her own complaints.

They became overwhelmed in close quarters at home, fighting battles in which both were complicit. When my parents argued, my mother fought back verbally. In retrospect, I see that both of my parents were alphas—in the face of a challenge, they didn't typically back down. In their power struggles, my father usually won, but my mother didn't let him win easily. Sometimes neither would relent because for one to win, the other was left to stew in resentment and frustration.

Mom and I were close. She confided in me about having had no options when things had started going south in their relationship. She told me she would take my sister Linda on walks to escape Bud's rages and wander aimlessly until it was safe to go back because she had no one to help her and nowhere else to go.

But she'd also been committed to the ideal of keeping the family together and appreciated Dad's role as a provider. Divorce was less common then, and it marked a single mother as a pariah. Lee had toughed it out on the emotional front in exchange for financial security for herself and her children.

SPILT MILK
AND SPEED EATING

G rowing up immersed in the battleground that was my parents' marriage, all the images, sounds, words, and behaviors I experienced were written indelibly in my mental archives, distorting my lexicon of love and relationships. There was no hugging, no kissing.

One evening, as my mother leaned over Dad complaining about some disrespectful act he'd perpetrated upon her, Dad seized a wide-mouth half-gallon milk bottle from the table, flicked off the cap with his thumb, and splashed her face with milk. As it caught her unaware, she sputtered and paused in her harangue. I saw her soul dim and deflate.

As a child, I absorbed these scenes as normal. The dynamics became a model for my sister and me: Love doesn't build up—it tears down. And though one might think as siblings Linda and I would have banded together to weather the discord, she was yet another alpha in the house. I was at the bottom of the heap, someone she could throw under the bus. Only later in life did I realize how toxic that environment was and how it warped our internalizations.

I cultivated speed eating so I could be excused from the table. Gulping and swallowing my food like a wild hyena on the Serengeti Plain, I would bound out of the kitchen, glad to be anywhere other than at ground zero of fever-pitched arguing. Alone in my bedroom, I'd replay each eruption and agonize over ways to disarm the tension in the house. If I could figure out and memorize the words, facial expressions, or actions that unleashed Dad's inner beast, I thought I could sidetrack the conversation or alter the path that ignited his self-righteous temper.

Years later when I went out to eat with people, most were amazed at the speed with which I consumed my food. I devoured a full dinner in minutes and, when finished, was anxious to be free from any table sitting. Though far from the torment of my childhood kitchen table, I couldn't even enjoy meals with my friends because of the conditioning I experienced as a child.

Another evening my mother asked Dad for permission to attend a Parent-Teacher Association (PTA) meeting about an upcoming bake sale. My father grunted his assent, and my mom and sister left for the meeting where my mother would be revered for her baking skills. She craved praise to assuage her insecurities and needed to prove to the community what a lovely, kind, and generous mother she was. She put considerable energy into hiding the strife at home and keeping up false appearances.

After Mom and Linda left, my father retired to the living room to read the paper, smoke a cigarette, and drink a glass of sherry. I interrupted his reverie and inquired meekly if I could go watch TV with Mrs. Timmerman, the sweet old lady who lived on the floor above us. He nodded his okay, so I bounded out to the back hall and up the rear staircase.

I knocked timidly at Mrs. T's door. She opened it and invited me in with a grandmotherly smile. After settling me in front of the black-and-white TV, she brought out milk and cookies and joined me in an armchair trip to the "perfect" world of American 1950s nightly programming. We laughed, we smiled, we oohed and aahed—each of us escaping our respective circumstances of solitude and fear. At Mrs. T's place, I let my guard down, slipping into relaxation and relishing the license to just be a kid.

Three or four TV shows later, Dad appeared, grabbed me by the scruff of my neck, and snatched me out of the chair, stunning Mrs. Timmerman. He threw me to the floor and kicked me toward the door to the back stairs. I crawled and skittered out, tumbling down the spiraling wood staircase. At the bottom, I got up and ran pell-mell into our kitchen and down the hall where I darted into my room, dove under the bed and curled tightly into a fetal position.

His booming voice informed me I was supposed to have been home by a certain time, now passed. He was enraged. Trembling, I chanted my well-worn mantra: I'm sorry, I'm sorry, I'm sorry.

After his fury ceased, he told me to get ready for bed. I slithered out, gathered myself, brushed my teeth fast, got in my pajamas, and huddled in my bed. I tried to close my mind to the dread.

The next morning, I awoke bruised and battered. With renewed determination to be on guard at all times, I read postures, faces, and voice levels like a meteorologist observes weather data to predict approaching tempests. At about that time in my life, I began having bouts of ulcerative colitis which baffled the doctors because I came from such an "upstanding" family.

Another evening after being excused from the dinner table, I couldn't contain my exuberance about a carnival I was told I could attend. I ran down the hallway into the living room. The energy I usually tried to stifle at home burst out of me, and I kicked up my heels with joy. One of my shoes came off and flew right through the front window into the night air, shattering the glass and the fragile household peace.

After a lengthy scolding seasoned with a dash of denigration, I was sent to my room. I was grounded indefinitely and would not be attending the festival. I went to bed with thoughts of shame, inadequacy, and regret that I hadn't been able to contain myself.

Where once Mom had come to my defense, over time she'd been worn down by battling with Dad. Now she tolerated his imperious disciplining and berating of me. She told me repeatedly that I had to learn things the hard way. Her conversations began with "I love you, but . . ." and continued with a litany of my wrongdoings.

My sister Linda, the first-born, was understandably her Daddy's girl, and she idolized him. She unwittingly mirrored his negative assessments of me. As for my father, I never heard him utter the word love. Anger and pique were more his kettle of calamari. I took all the abuse because that was my role.

When our parents deemed that our castigation hadn't been sufficient, we were threatened with The Strap. Big Bad Bud would go to his bureau, pull out a rattlesnake-patterned leather belt, fold it over, and slowly slap the palm of his hand with it. Then he'd ask us our "favorite" question:

"Do you want The Strap?"

In our house, not only were we hit, but we were hit in anger.

One day, Bud pounded a nail into the kitchen wall and hung the belt there. It made for easier access and served as a visual reminder to my sister and me. Within view of The Strap, we would drink chocolate milk with a straw, blow bubbles hard until the milk spilled over the glass, and giggle with whatever restraint we could muster amid our childish abandon. Lee or Bud, unamused, would ask through pursed lips, "Do you want The Strap?"

Given that I'd inherited my parents' unrestrained natures and knacks for sarcasm, I sometimes fantasized about responding, "You betcha! The first thing I wanted to do when I woke up this morning was to get whacked across my bottom with a rattlesnake belt. *Please, please* give it to me Mom and Dad."

But I would bite my tongue instead. I was frequently instructed to "Wipe that smirk off your face." The command didn't have the desired effect. I couldn't keep a straight face—their demand made my smirk even smirkier.

DUKE

About a block from our house on Tibbetts Avenue was a fraternity house affiliated with nearby Rensselaer Polytechnic Institute. In my excursions around the neighborhood, I came upon an intimidating yet beautiful caramel-fawn dog at the frat. He had the chest of a weightlifter and the waist of a wasp. His snout was black as coal.

Chained to a steel rod pounded into the untended dirt yard, he barked at me like he was Cerberus, the three-headed dog of Greek mythology who guarded the underworld. Though I was only six years old, I was undeterred—I was more afraid of The Strap than the dog.

I inched nearer, and the dog lowered his deep bark to a growl. I sensed he wouldn't hurt me, so I approached even closer. The magnificent boxer started wagging his tail like crazy. As I got within his reach, he came to me and nuzzled my chest. I must have hugged and petted him for some time because when I heard my mom hollering for me to come home for dinner, I noticed my shirt looked like a soaked dishrag (boxers typically have endless supplies of drool). I skipped home filled with the dog's affection and exuberance. I had just met a new friend who would love me forever and never be disappointed in me.

Taking along good kitchen scraps, I visited him as often as possible because I knew he was lonely. All he wanted was to love and to be loved in return—the same as myself. I likewise felt chained to a stake in my family's dysfunctional diorama, and I just wanted to be free to run and leap and make mistakes and be forgiven.

Sometimes the dog's collar would break, and he would find his way to our house. If I was home, I'd play with him for as long as I could before Mom or Dad took him back to his forlorn hell. Hooked to a chain is not a good life for any creature—when you take away their flight, they have to resort to growling and barking to protect themselves.

One day when he'd gotten loose, he was hit by a car on Tibbetts Avenue. Thankfully he wasn't gravely injured, but he needed a trip to the vet to remove some metal from his cheek. Concerned for the dog's welfare, my parents talked with the student who owned the dog and offered to pay for the dog's treatment.

They also asked if our family could keep him as our own. The guy agreed, aware that he didn't have time for the dog. He gave us the dog's American Kennel Club (AKC) papers. The purebred had a fancy registered name, but we called him Duke, and the first thing my mom did was train him not to pee or poo in the house.

The author and Duke, circa 1954

Duke was so happy to be free that he pranced and bounced like a ballet dancer on a pogo stick. Despite the fierce demeanor he displayed when safeguarding our family, Duke was a gentle soul who loved kids. My older sister and I were thrilled. We had an enthusiastic four-legged pal who was always game to play.

My first therapist, Duke became my solace. As I sat with him, stroked his head, and told him my woes, his rapt attention to my words soothed me. He lifted the anchor of sadness off my shoulders with his kind eyes and cocked head. His responsive posturing exuded an empathy that made me feel understood and worthy. He loved me no matter what stupid blunder I'd performed or what mischief I'd gotten into. He was loyal and true, an endless source of light to which I was drawn.

When I would return to my chores and to the weighty expectations placed on me to be the son my dad wanted, I walked a little easier knowing that Duke liked me just the way I was. He also gave me hope, as if he was reassuring me that, like him, someday I would be released from my constraining chain and set free to find my own safe haven.

In the snowy New York winters, we kids built snow forts and tunneled through snowdrifts. A buddy of mine and I once dug tunnels in the depression of a drainage culvert and excitedly crawled way down into some drifts, oblivious to danger. The roof of the tunnel collapsed on us, but before we could panic, we heard frantic digging and then saw Duke's black snout and his warm brown eyes appear. He licked us and stayed close until we crawled back up to the surface.

Every summer Duke came with us to Vermont where we vacationed. He would accompany us as we explored every nook and cranny in the deep woods. Duke would chase chipmunks, squirrels, and the occasional deer, but he never wandered far and always came back quickly because he was steadfast in his role as our protector. In return, we made sure he never saw a chain again.

FERMÉ LA BOUCHE

A head of me in school, my sister was an A-plus scholar. I was a C-D-F student who became the attention-seeking class clown. Loud was the tenor of my household, and I bore that with me to school. I excelled at making my peers and friends laugh with my incessant yakking and slapstick comedy. I told jokes and goofed around. Unfortunately, in the process, I disrupted teachers' lessons. But at school, no one hit me. Because I craved affection, I went through much of life in the guise of a lighthearted joker.

I took French class with Mrs. Mercier who also was beleaguered by my constant interruption and acting out. I heard the phrase *fermé la bouche* (close your mouth) so often in that class that, to this day, I think of it whenever I hear someone say "shut up."

But Mrs. Mercier must have taken psychology in college, for she had the temerity to question my family life which, of course, shamed my parents. I don't remember the details, but my dad was furious. My recollection is that he drove her out of the system. Her promising career in our school district was derailed. After all, who would people believe — a respected lawyer or a naive young teacher who was too big for her britches? She learned the hard way what happened when you advocated for a kid from a "good" family.

I felt bad for the pretty auburn-haired lady who attempted to go to bat for an abused child against a system that held my father up as a bastion of society. I've often wondered what happened to the outsider who dared question what was behind our family's curtain of privilege.

When school wasn't in session, the neighborhood kids played pickup baseball at the high school fields. One day when not enough kids showed up to make a game, I crawled under the fence bordering the fields into some woods at the edge of a marsh where older kids hung out and smoked cigarettes. I was eleven, and not long after I got there, a teenager put me in a headlock and wouldn't let go. He then sexually assaulted me.

It was quickly over, and he released me. I made for the fence, slid under it, and ran for home. I didn't tell anyone in my family because I was certain I would be blamed for going somewhere I shouldn't have gone for a smoke I shouldn't have wanted. I'd be shamed even more than I already was. So I kept the burden to myself, adding to my browbeaten spirit. The good news was our family moved within the year to an East Side neighborhood far from that tough guy's turf.

Later in high school, I was preyed upon by a teacher when we were on an overnight field trip, but I was able to escape the situation before any assault occurred. Once again, I never told a soul about it. In hindsight, I believe being pushed around daily by my father made me susceptible to bullies who pegged me—rightly—as a victim. My face expressed my insecurity, and it drew predators to me.

At our new home on the East Side, the kitchen table was situated next to a bay window overlooking the backyard. Bud liked to sit at an end close to the window's wide ledge because that's where his beloved radio sat. Dad was the only one allowed to touch it—we didn't dare change the station.

One spring evening, we gulped dinner there. Bud and sixteen-year-old Linda sat at one side of the table, with me, twelve years old, and my mom sitting at the other side. Four-year-old Carol (she was an "oops" baby) was placed at the end sticking out between the kitchen and the formal dining room. Beyond the window, a cherry tree bloomed with pink blossoms.

Bud wound down a diatribe aimed at me about my latest blunders. As he paused for a breath, my angelic-looking kid sister, normally quiet, interjected, "Why don't you leave the no-good, rotten, mother-f***ing sonofabitch alone?"

The kid had been paying attention.

Everyone froze in shock, anticipating Bud's explosion. But instead he burst out laughing at the unexpected challenge from a most unlikely source. We all followed suit with relief. My heart swelled because someone had stood up for me.

Years passed, and because of my ongoing poor behavior in school, my father sent me to a boarding school when I was sixteen years old. He hoped they might reform me. I flunked out by the end of my first term in December. Merry Christmas Dad!

Once I was back home and reenrolled in public high school, my desperate parents—typically opposed to psychology because they held to deeply-rooted traditions of keeping a stiff upper lip and pulling yourself up by the bootstrap—took me to a psychiatrist who, in private, instructed me in ways to stand up for myself.

But the fear of my father was so strongly embedded that I found it too daunting to confront his authority. Dad's disposition and law training combined to make his bullying and interrogations razor-sharp. I was a kid, not a defendant, but it seemed I'd been charged with the crime of being a disappointment. I wasn't the son my father wanted or expected me to be.

Clearly, law school was not in my future. But I showed athletic potential. At school, I now spent time in organized sports and gained some meager self-confidence. Come winter, I enjoyed ice hockey on Belden's Pond. No one in my family praised me for my athletic achievements, one of the few areas in which I applied myself with good results. Playing a sport released my pent-up emotional energy and generated endorphins. During vigorous exercise, my need for air stifled my perpetual chatter, providing those around me with much-needed relief. In high school, I lettered in soccer and golf.

Despite not having any faith in me, Dad tried to mold me into a great golfer, a last-ditch effort to fulfill an ambition he'd put aside. My father had played golf and developed into a talented amateur, winning the Vermont State Amateur Championship in 1934 and 1936. In 1949, he was, to my understanding, the last person to best Julius Boros before the latter turned professional.

Dad could have gone pro but stayed with law as his career because tournament purses at the time wouldn't pay what he considered to be a secure income for raising a family. Anyone following professional golf saw that change dramatically over the years.

Bud never consulted Lee about that unilateral decision in their past. She knew how to make do with little and might have been willing to take a chance with life married to a professional golfer. Law was not a practice my father relished, but he did it well. And he enjoyed golfing on the weekends as an amateur for the rest of his life. He won tournaments at the Country Club of Troy and at local and regional courses. I wonder what he thought—tuned in to golf on TV as tourney purses grew—watching the pro golfers doing what he might have done.

Though I was a good junior golfer and played on the high school team, my own weaknesses, such as ADHD and poor impulse control, made for a shaky foundation on which to build a decent amateur golfer, let alone a pro. If I could have been diagnosed and placed on the right medication, it might have helped me with various aspects of my life, but at the time, golf wasn't suited to me.

I simply didn't have it in me to hit balls on the golf course until my hands bled, which my father alleged *he* did. When he would tell me that, I'd respond with a wiseass retort. Stunned by my irreverence, he would bristle, tighten his jaw, and set his face into the stern countenance I was so accustomed to. His inflexible teaching method of yelling at me after every bad shot was not constructive. It only made my golf game worse and exacerbated our poor relationship.

What's the saying: Man plans, God laughs?

THE NOZZLE INCIDENT

Mom and we kids spent summers at Lake Dunmore, a small lake nestled up against Mount Moosalamoo in Vermont. Our cottage was surrounded by woods that I loved to explore. Dad would drive us up in June or July and then return to Troy. He would visit on weekends throughout the season when he had the time. Life was easier for me when he couldn't make it.

Dad insisted everybody be completely packed the night before we left to drive up there. He wanted us ready to go when he finished breakfast—no farting around with last-minute efforts. On one morning of departure, I settled into the Chevy's back seat with my sisters. Mom was sitting up front. We'd all made it before the appointed time, so the day was looking good.

We waited for Dad in anticipation of getting on the road. House doors slammed. We held our collective breath. He came out the last door and down the porch steps with all the nuance of a tornado. Arriving red-faced, blood pressure cranked to the max, he bent over and peered into the back seat through the open window.

"Has anyone seen the brass nozzle for the garden hose that I purchased *brand new* this week?" He was barely keeping a lid on the steaming pot of his irritation.

"No, sir," we chorused, pinned against the seat by his pressurized persona.

"Well," he began in a prosecutorial tone suggesting one of us must be lying because, of course, *he* couldn't have misplaced it, "it's missing from the shelf in the back hall, and we are not going anywhere until it's found."

Then he blew. Dad vented expletives and ordered us out of the car to find the damn nozzle. We scrambled out. Tasked with a mission that must be accomplished before we could leave the godforsaken driveway, I scurried about the yard and the garage, keeping my eyes peeled for the cherished hunk of cast metal.

Mom asked Dad why he needed the nozzle because the plants had been watered and the birdbath was freshly filled.

"That's not the point, dammit! Everything must be in its place, or we can't go," he insisted, then added dismissively, "you *know* that, Lee," as if bewildered that she would even have to ask.

His irrational, unyielding stance loomed over us, a force we could not defeat but only temporarily put at bay by finding the nozzle. Mom resigned to the fiasco, just one more in a string of aggravations.

After searching for twenty minutes, Dad commanded us to get back in the car, and we did so with trepidation because we were about to be in an enclosed space with a raving lunatic. My sisters and I shrunk down in the back seat.

Nobody mentioned finding the brass piece. I assumed he'd discovered it hidden in some obscure place he'd forgotten about and was too chagrined to admit it. As he backed the car out of the driveway past the birch tree (that I would in the future crease repeatedly when I got my driver's permit), he muttered about how he worked his ass off to provide for us and all we did was squander his efforts with our irresponsibility. The lecture we'd heard many times before about life's inequities rolled off his tongue and bounced off the chrome accents of the Bel Air's interior.

We stayed quiet as we rode along back roads through forests and pastures dotted with cows. Dad wound down. Mom craned her neck around and urged us silently via imploring looks to hold it together long enough to get there without poking the bear back into rage mode. Her face was part stern and part apologetic.

Linda perused her teen magazines, and I read comic books. Between us and standing on the hump over the drive shaft that ran down the middle of the car, Carol rested her arms and head on the top of the front bench seat (this was before seat belt laws). For this practice, she had acquired the nickname Humpy. Soon it would dawn on Mom and Dad that they must put the kibosh on that moniker, but at the time, it was silly and had a nice ring to it: Humpy Russell.

We crossed our legs, held our bladders, and restrained from blurting, "Are we there yet?"

Our cottage was about a half mile down a dirt road that wound through evergreen trees. When we pulled into our lot, we could see the lake bordered by scattered clumps of blueberry bushes. Across the water beyond our weathered dock, Mount Moosalamoo rose against the sky. My buddies and I liked to hike up there and eat peanut butter and jelly sandwiches in a cave once used by Ethan Allen and the Green Mountain Boys in the 1700s.

After rains, I raced out of the cottage into the woods to search for the bright orange newts that stood out against the dark brown forest floor. On Saturday nights, we walked dirt roads to the roller-skating rink where we would glide around and around to organ music with friends. We walked back home scuffing up dust, our flashlights illuminating the way through the scary trees of pitch-black nights.

Sometimes we played miniature golf on the other side of Lake Dunmore. If you scored a hole-in-one on the last hole, you earned a free round, a fabulous feat to us kids.

We water-skied behind our skiff that was outfitted with an 18 horsepower Johnson outboard motor that could barely drag adults out of the water. We fished with lures off the dock and with bobbers from the boat. It was a glorious time to be active outside on "wild" adventures in the fresh air and sun, excited about each day, and free from the fear of being cornered and yelled at.

WHEN I LEFT

L ittle did I know as a kid how long I would reside in an insufferable house of alphas before I could spread my wings and fly away as the universe intended. When I ended up with a low draft number in the early 1970s, the opportunity to get *really* far away from my parents presented itself. I did not wait. I signed up, expecting to be sent to Vietnam after basic training. I was posted to South Korea instead.

Looking in my metaphorical rearview mirror, there are lessons I learned in my parents' house:

—Parental love (or rather, attention) was loud and critical.

—Parenting children properly meant no coddling, spoiling, or befriending.

—Children were to be seen and not heard.

—Fear was a motivator.

—Hardship built character.

—Crying is forbidden.

As their individual dreams disintegrated, my parents had reinvested their hopes in raising a family. But their incompatibilities, combined with their ignorance about managing anger, resolving conflict, and how to express loving familial relations, soured the family bonds. Power struggles and bitterness poisoned their original joy.

They had played out their stormy scenes on our family stage. I've realized that they'd most likely been immersed in similar dynamics in their own childhoods. They were unable to break the cycle of drama and abuse. They couldn't pass along to me and my sisters ways to constructively deal with dysfunction. We would have to learn that on our own.

Some things, however, my parents did well: They provided us with shelter, clothes, abundant food, and education. Now—despite the negative parts of their parenting—I see that they expressed their love through work and daily duties. I believe they did the best they could, and they never quit.

Occasionally, I still have lingering guilt for the abuse my mother received from my father when she tried to protect me from his wrath. I've thought that if I'd been smarter, I could have defused it. But I've realized that as a kid I'd been powerless.

When I left behind that house of fear and control, I promised myself I would never do to anyone what had been done to me. I also swore that I would never let anyone subject me to threats—to the point that I was subconsciously hypervigilant to conflict. It triggered my emotions, causing distress and an intense fight-or-flight response. Thankfully I've learned to walk away from such stimulation.

NETHER-LAIR

Honorably discharged from the US Army, I returned home to upstate New York. I had just two weeks there before heading to Franklin, Massachusetts, to attend Dean College (then Dean Junior College). It was fitting that their mascot was a bulldog.

My classes ran most weekday mornings, so in the afternoons, I scouted the area and discovered a reputable boarding and training kennel—Nether-Lair—in nearby Wrentham. I landed a job there and worked after classes, primarily teaching obedience with the daycare dogs dropped off on weekdays.

On the weekends, we offered sessions coaching dog owners and their canines together. I also trained a marijuana-detecting dog and a tracking dog for the

Massachusetts State Police. I was young, fit, confident, and naively fearless of all dogs.

Curiously, my talent in dog training and my flawed childhood were interrelated. Dogs communicate using various nonverbal vocalizations and a diverse repertoire of body language. In my upbringing, I most certainly had been well-versed in paying attention to nonverbal cues, albeit of the human variety.

One day that autumn, Nether-Lair's proprietor, Jack Cowley, wanted someone to leash up an attack-trained German shepherd mix and run the dog through a review of basic commands. Jack was selling the shepherd as a yard dog to a tire shop owner coming by that day.

Inflated with the hubris of a twenty-one-year-old, I retrieved Bad Duke and worked him in the sit, stay, come, down, and heel commands in the front yard. He balked when I commanded Down. I pressed my foot down on the leash—connected to Bad Duke's chain collar—while issuing the stern verbal correction No.

Once he was under control (or so I thought), I stepped off the leash. The dog leapt at me. I pulled his collar and tried to get him off balance, thinking that was how I was supposed to handle an alpha dog. But he managed to connect with me, biting my hands and forearms. Tightening his collar with my right arm, I lifted him off the ground briefly. Within seconds he stopped attacking. I released him and yelled Sit. To my surprise, he did.

Going around to the kennel's back entrance, I handed the dog over to another trainer with blood still dripping down my arms. Bad Duke was delivered to his new owner that day. Jack didn't find out about the bites until after.

I'd gone straight from the kennel to the nearest emergency room where I was disinfected, stitched up, and given propoxyphene pills which are now-banned opioid painkillers. I took a few days off.

As my arms and hands throbbed during the following days, I reevaluated my technique. In hindsight, all I'd ever done with Bad Duke prior to the obedience run-through was agitate him while he was chained to a stake—the intent when training attack dogs back then was to make them distrust anyone but their owner. Clearly, I'd done an excellent job with Bad Duke because he sure didn't trust me!

Given I'd been one of the staff assigned to provoke Bad Duke, it was probably a bad idea to have me do his review. But when doing so, I should have been more patient and praised him for his heel, sit, come, and stay. My physical attempt to out-muscle and dominate him didn't work. On a positive note, I survived the lesson with all fingers intact.

The ultimate adjustments I made from that attack were to keep my overconfidence in check and to pay strict attention to a dog's posturing and behavior. Posturing is the position of the dog's ears and tail. If the ears are back and flattened tightly to the head, the dog feels cornered. If the ears are up and moving back and forth, and if the dog's mouth is tightly closed or its tail is tucked under its body, the dog is tense, scared, and on alert.

A dog standing straight with its head held high and fur all fluffed out could be in a dominant stance that might mean the dog is prepared to attack. Anyone who owns—or wants to own—a dog should learn about a dog's posturing and their body language in general. Ignoring or lacking knowledge of the signals a dog displays could lead to mishap and regret.

I continued employment at Nether-Lair until graduating from Dean with a degree in Business Administration and a minor in Criminalistics. I trained many dogs and was never bitten by a dog there again.

GONE WEST

After graduating from Dean, I again returned to New York. I would need money to open my own dog-handling business, but training for someone else's kennel wouldn't pay much. So I went to work for a bank, and unfortunately learned rather quickly that a desk job wasn't for me. I needed to be outdoors and moving.

The American West appealed to me, so I packed my few belongings and moved to Colorado. In Denver, I was enticed by offers to work in modeling and sales. I explored those other paths for a time.

On the journey to finding my independent self, I stumbled forward and backward, bolting at any seismic mental activity that reactivated my fears. Inwardly a piece of work in the outward guise of a carefree comic, I craved love and affection.

When I started to sense those feelings from women I was attracted to, I would get scared and push them away because the voice in my head said I didn't deserve it. I'd internalized being a disappointment and a failure, someone unworthy of love. In running from positive, intimate relationships, I hurt a lot of folks.

I came to realize how much reflection on my past was required for me to acknowledge my issues and transform my behaviors. I wanted to know what it was like to sit with friends at a meal and find it to be relaxing. Had I been missing one of life's simple pleasures?

I wrestled with the archival tapes that played over and over in my head telling me I would never amount to anything. The destructive mindset and negative habits instilled in my brain were a bunch of bull—lies hindering my search for love, happiness, and a peaceful way to be in this world.

Because of my concerns and the resulting blowups of anger I'd had as an adult, I sought counseling. At a Veterans Affairs (VA, formerly Veterans Administration) facility, I once asked a shrink if my anger was caused by learned behavior or genetic make-up. He replied calmly with a pretentious, vague "yes" that he probably thought clever, but he failed to elaborate on his answer—that genetics and learned behavior can go hand in hand, as we now understand. His cerebral, condescending manner annoyed me—it evoked flashbacks of my father's patronizing demeanor.

I moved on from that guy, looking elsewhere for a therapist I could connect with positively. In the Denver area, I found and met with an awesome counselor, the late Rosa Mazone, who taught me much about finding peace and learning to love myself.

I ripped out those critical tapes in my head. I pulled a surgically sharp scalpel out of my inner resolve and began cutting out my triggers that unleashed outsized, knee-jerk reactions. Rosa and I worked together to establish supportive messages that I could tell myself and to replace old, conditioned outbursts with constructive expressions of my emotions—expressions that supported healthy relationships.

She encouraged me to continue the "reparenting," and I took her wisdom to heart. Rosa was a bright, compassionate light who guided me—and many others—out of the dark depths of self-hatred.

Over a decade or so, I worked my way around to southern California, reveling in the wide horizons and heat of the Southwest. I advertised in a local Pasadena paper as a dog trainer, finally making time to do what I loved. Working with puppies and rescues mostly, I would go to a client's house where I would leash, walk, and train my furry students.

BAD DOGS WITH MIDNIGHT AND AIKO

I n the early 1990s, I relocated to Phoenix, Arizona, where I worked for the largest dog training outfit in the metro area. It was a lucrative operation run by a successful but abusive businessman. Working in the vicinity of someone who abused others didn't appeal to me, so I put my energy and drive into quietly gaining more knowledge through practice.

Within two years, I launched my own company, Bad Dogs, that I ran out of a two-bedroom condominium I shared with Rena, my then companion. I did house calls training dogs at the owners' homes, but I also boarded up to ten dogs in addition to our own two dogs.

How did I do this in a condo? It worked for several reasons. The unit—including an attached garage—was entirely enclosed. There was a dog door to an outdoor patio in the back yard that was surrounded by high walls. All the side-by-side units were likewise: No one could see into anyone else's house or yard, and the homes had good sound insulation. It was a bedroom community, so most people who lived there were gone during the day. I also offered free pickup and delivery of dogs to eliminate car traffic to and from the house.

Additionally, it was important to consider the dispositions of the dogs I would board. Many species, including wolves and dogs, live in groups (packs) that establish social hierarchies. The individuals making up a group fall into various roles or positions. In the pack structure, there is a top alpha (leader), maybe a milder alpha or two that are content to submit to the top alpha, omegas (bottom of the pack), and betas (in between alphas and omegas).

Members of a canine unit naturally tend toward a level based on the personality they're born with; however, for some dogs their group role or level might vary depending on their breed and the pack they are a part of.

Assessing the temperaments of potential boarders to see if they were aggressive toward humans or other dogs was crucial for me and the dogs under my care. Understandably, most of my training courses were taken by clients seeking help with their domineering, assertive dogs with—you guessed it—alpha temperaments. But given that the condo lacked sufficient space for separate dog runs, I wasn't able to board the alpha dogs routinely.

Doing so involved too much risk with pack harmony. One mistake could decimate my business, so I took in dogs with predominantly beta dispositions—the easy-going dogs that got along well with others. Occasionally, I would accommodate an alpha or two, but only if I knew them to be well-trained.

I also had a hard-and-fast rule that all my boarders had to be spayed or neutered by six months of age, because females in heat and unneutered males with high testosterone could derail my operation faster than a dog could lift its leg and squirt. Luckily, I was able to avert an impending disaster involving an unneutered English bulldog puppy named Spuds, who I boarded for a Phoenix Suns athlete at the Olympic Trials. I had to crate Spuds and keep a close eye on him when he needed to be uncrated.

Rena tolerated me bringing my four-legged clients into our pack on a rotating basis. In the pecking order of the pack's core, Rena was top alpha, and I was the number-two alpha. Midnight—a beta-female, and without a doubt, one of the sweetest, smartest dogs I've ever worked with—was next in command, my first lieutenant so to speak. Aiko, a beta-male golden retriever-collie mix, who I considered my second lieutenant of the pack, ranked above the boarders but was subordinate to Rena, me, and Midnight.

Rena and I first met after she contacted me to train Midnight, her Labrador-shepherd-chow mix. It was one of my easiest assignments because Midnight and I simply clicked. Rena's mother, Ruth, was a kind, generous matriarch who taught me how to hug. She was like a mom to me, one who physically demonstrated affection with ample hugging.

Midnight

Midnight had blue-black fur with a question-mark tail that wagged back and forth like a metronome keeping time at *tempo vivace*. She picked up obedience quickly. A true beta, Midnight was a lover and a player. She became our canine queen of the pack—a natural at knowing how and when to play her roles.

With her friendly disposition, she greeted all boarders that came to stay with us at Bad Dogs—puppies and older dogs alike—at the door with a twinkle in her eyes, a gently wagging tail, and a soft lick from her bubble-gum pink tongue. The perfect hostess, she would lead them into the house and make them feel comfortable as they entered our inner sanctum.

Aiko had been rescued by a young woman who nursed him through a serious bout of tick fever. As he recovered, he became a lot to handle. She called me to see if he could be helped to overcome his many fears resulting from past abuse. As far as she knew, he had never bitten anyone, however if he had, I still would have been willing to assess him.

Laws concerning injuries from dog bites vary among states, counties, and other jurisdictions. In Arizona, dogs didn't get "one free bite" with no consequences. Arizona had a strict liability law that applied if a dog bit someone: A dog's owner was liable for any injuries or damages their dog caused if a victim could show that their injury resulted from the dog attack. An exception existed only if the dog owner could prove that the victim's actions provoked the otherwise benign dog, either intentionally or in some cases, unintentionally. Therefore, it benefited a dog owner to be attentive to, and responsible for, their dog's behavior.

If a dog broke the skin of a victim it bit and the matter was reported to animal control, the dog was quarantined and tested for rabies. Medical staff who treated a person for a serious bite wound were typically required to report it. Assessing a dog for rabies was imperative, especially if a victim wasn't familiar with the dog and its record of shots.

If healthy, the dog would be released to its owner if the bite was a first offense, but if the dog had a record of two or more bites—thus showing a pattern of aggression—animal control could seize the dog and have it euthanized. Animal control officers were trying to prevent further attacks and injuries by problem dogs.

If a dog tested positive for rabies, it was usually put down, since there is no known cure for rabies. Thus it's crucial to have your veterinarian vaccinate your pet for rabies, a vaccine that must be renewed periodically.

I was among the minority of trainers to work with dogs who had bitten a person. Many trainers viewed it as a waste of their time to work with an animal they considered "blooded." I didn't see it that way. To me it was worth trying, maybe because I was the poster child of second and third chances.

So I had driven up to Cave Creek twenty-five miles north of Phoenix to evaluate Aiko. By approaching the dog in various ways and observing his reactions, I determined that most likely he'd been hit by a man wearing a trucker type hat and kicked from behind as well. Given the intense and persistent sun in Arizona, I often wore such a hat when out and happened to be wearing one when I met Aiko. When I first approached him, Aiko growled and bared some teeth. When I removed the hat and put it away, he relaxed, stopping his vocalization and dental display.

Using only my correction tone, a nylon slip collar, and constant praise for positive responses, I kept Aiko from freezing up with fear. I gently put him in a sit, then down-stay position, praising him all the way. From there I practiced slow movements of my arm coming toward his head from above. As my hand neared, he cringed, but as I turned the motion into a gentle stroke on his head, he learned that my hand wouldn't hurt him. While circling him, I would lift my foot slowly (formerly a threat to him), all the while lavishing him with cheerful singsong good boys. This process helped Aiko gradually overcome his dread around men.

Within weeks of being worked from five to twenty minutes at a time, Aiko no longer flinched but instead reached up for the physical praise of being stroked on his head, neck, and flanks. When we finished our routine, I would squat and call him to me. He'd come and sit perfectly between my legs so I could give him good, loving pets with plenty of physical and verbal praise. Dogs live for praise. Aiko ate it up, shedding his fear in leaps and bounds.

Once I'd won his trust, I worked with Aiko on polishing his basic obedience skills. Like Midnight, he performed with me so naturally it was as though we were one choreographed unit instead of two separate beings. Aiko's owner was pleased with the results. As much as I hated leaving that dog, he'd mastered everything the woman wanted him to do. When I graduated him and said my goodbyes, I told the client if she ever couldn't keep him to please give me a call because I would adopt Aiko in a heartbeat.

One Saturday several months later, I got a call from her asking me if I still wanted Aiko. I was on my way back from Tucson where I'd worked with some huskies for the Arizona Siberian Husky Rescue and Adoption (ASHRA) organization. It had been a long hot day—I was tired and irritable. Though I wasn't in the mood to pass by home and drive all the way to the other side of Phoenix, I didn't want to give the woman a chance to change her mind. Aiko and I had created a powerful bond during training.

Aiko

When I got there, the young lady explained that her new boyfriend didn't get along with Aiko, so the dog had to go. I bit my tongue thinking she would be better off ditching the boyfriend, but if that was her attitude, I was happy to take Aiko. I thought he and Midnight would make a great team in our pack. Aiko was so happy to see me, vocalizing his delight. The woman released him, and he ran straight to me and sat. I wrapped my arms around him. My sour mood evaporated, replaced by a surge of pure loving energy.

The woman gave me his crate, leash, and toys, and I loaded them into the Pathfinder with Aiko. We headed for home where we were greeted by Midnight who welcomed Aiko like he was a dear long-lost brother. Aiko smiled, pranced, and settled at my feet in a down-stay position. He had many undiscovered gifts that I would come to know.

I've trekked desert trails, mountain paths, and even bushwhacked tracks through thick vegetated areas with Midnight and Aiko off-leash, keeping my eyes on the horizon while routinely reining in those two loyal dogs to my side. They responded instantly to my commands to come, Aiko with much more speed because he was so fleet of foot. Midnight obeyed, but her style was to amble her way over to me, smiling all the way but rarely hurried.

Hiking with Midnight made my heart sing. She enjoyed every step she took and taught me to savor being in the present. The first time I walked her off-leash in the desert in late spring, she darted from bush to bush as if chasing something, but I'd be damned if I saw anything. After much scrutiny, I discovered she was chasing geckos, tiny lizards that burst forth when the temperatures climbed above eighty-five. Her playful side made me laugh.

When I worked with puppy boarders and took them hiking, I would drop their leashes so they could have some freedom. If they wandered too far from the pack, I'd dispatch Aiko to retrieve them. He would run out, grab a leash, shake it like a correction, and then lead them back to me. Then I'd pick up the leash, praise him, and heel the returned puppy while Aiko ran out to get another one. After corralling them all, he would patrol the outskirts of the moving pack, swaggering with his collie tail all fluffed, buffed, and puffed.

Once when walking in the vicinity of Northern Avenue and Eighteenth Street just west of the Arizona SR-51 freeway through Phoenix, Aiko and Midnight flushed a coyote off a rabbit kill. The coyote dashed up and out of the ravine, his muzzle dark red with blood, with Midnight and Aiko in hot pursuit. Nervous that the coyote might attack one of the dogs, I recalled my packmates. They broke off the chase and returned to me with the swagger of adrenaline-filled predators. They had operated as a pack with a cohesion that astounded me.

Those two dogs served me well through thick and thin for many years, and my love for them filled me daily. They were essential to the exercise and training of the dogs in my care, to modeling good pack behavior in the house, and for assisting me with a larger group when we went on daily hikes with all the boarders in our expanded pack. With them I continued my journey learning about dogs, their interactions with humans, and how best to train and care for them—topics I cover in Part II of this book with tips on developing a responsible, constructive, and rewarding relationship with a dog.

Part II

PIERCE H RUSSELL JR

STUFFED VS. REAL

Who wouldn't fall in love with an adorable puppy, or smile watching friendly canines at play? Humans love dogs. But before you take the plunge into dog ownership, keep in mind that owning a dog is a substantial, prolonged commitment. Most dogs live about eight to fifteen years, and some live longer depending on their breed and health—even as old as twenty.

This highlights one of the downsides to owning a dog: Their life is much too short compared to that of their human owner. It's tough to watch a dog decline in its last years or months, and it's a labor of love to hang in there as calmly and lovingly as you can when they can't do what they used to do. It's heartbreaking to lose our dear, ever-faithful companions who have loved us without complaint.

For a happy, healthy life, dogs require not only food, water, and shelter but also love, attention, regular exercise, and veterinary care. The needs of your dog are *your* responsibility. Are you up to the task? What kind of companion animal will you commit to: stuffed or real?

If you get a dog but won't feed it in a timely manner, exercise it daily, train it consistently so it learns what you expect, and praise it when it behaves correctly, then you're wasting one of life's precious riches. Millions of real dogs are discarded every year in the US—please don't contribute to such a dismal statistic. It would be better to go online or to a toy store and buy a plushie. Seriously.

If you didn't already know, don't buy puppies purely because they're cute. Within a year they'll be teenagers and by two years they'll be morphing into adults. It's a time of great growth and transition. If you plan to purchase a purebred puppy, do your research on dog breeds—both the individual breed and the breed group it belongs to.

For example, the beagle breed is part of the hound group, border collies are part of the herding group, Labrador retrievers belong to the sporting group, etc. In each of the seven AKC breed groups, member breeds have some similar attributes and functions based on the purpose for which the dogs in a group were originally bred.

Breeds have been created over decades, in some cases centuries, for specific reasons, and you need to know what behaviors and traits have been bred into the dog.

Inbred traits are not behaviors you can train out of your purebred dog. They are automatic responses set in your dog's DNA, so learn about a breed's qualities, characteristics, health issues, and size as an adult. On the internet, you can find many breed profiles and tools (do a browser search on "dog breed selector") that help you choose a breed appropriate for you and your family—use those tools. When you have identified some breeds you're interested in, it's a great idea to attend a few dog shows where you can observe dogs from specific breeds and talk to dog owners about the breed they own and show.

Don't pick a dog or breed simply for looks. If you go with a purebred, select a reputable breeder such as one registered with an established breed association. Don't buy a puppy from a puppy mill—you don't want to support people who breed purely for profit and who have no concern for the health of the pups.

For less money than a purebred puppy from a breeder will cost, breed rescue groups can introduce you to purebred dogs that need a forever home. These organizations are excellent resources for learning about the breed you're interested in.

There are also plenty of wonderful dogs waiting at shelters to be adopted. When you go to the animal shelter to pick out a dog or puppy, seek out an animal you sense you have a connection with. Inquire with the staff about a particular dog's breed or breed mix. Due to their greater genetic diversity, mixed-breed dogs generally have fewer health issues than purebreds.

Consider a dog's temperament when choosing a puppy or adult pet. Determining your dog's disposition, and where that fits in the ranks of canine social order, means you can be better prepared about their behavior, development, and appropriate training. Knowledge is power!

With puppies and dogs new to me, I've always assessed their dispositions first, factoring in their breed or breed mix, before conducting any training. On my initial visit to a client's house, I evaluate the puppy or dog in the owner's presence and perform the alpha/beta test to determine if the canine is a leader or a follower.

Whether they know it or not, most people should adopt dogs with beta dispositions because betas are followers, not boundary pushers and testers. Some people think they want an alpha dog but don't necessarily understand what's involved with handling one over the long haul. Alphas are genetically driven to strive to be top dog in the pack. This means they will forever be challenging *you* for pack leadership, especially if you show any signs of weakness.

To test a puppy, I roll them onto their back while praising them and check my watch as I hold them down with one hand. If the pup lies submissive for thirty seconds, it's a true beta, basically a lover and a player.

If the puppy struggles to right itself by kicking, wriggling, twisting, and scratching before thirty seconds are up, then it's an alpha. How soon the puppy starts struggling to regain their footing indicates how much of an alpha they are—the quicker the squirming and resisting begins, the stronger an alpha you're dealing with.

To evaluate adult dogs, I observe their behavior and physical posturing around other dogs and people. Alpha dogs will posture standing straight and tall with their chests up, holding their tails straight or up, and barking when strangers approach. The fur around their necks may stand up in a ruff so they look like a little lion. The alphas won't give others any ground and may even charge forward as they bark. If a person runs away from them, alphas may give chase.

Dogs with beta temperaments will bark and *back up* when strangers approach. They don't posture with their chests or tails up and out, and they don't generally chase strangers.

Shelter staff can help you assess a dog's temperament and specific needs. Tell them about any concerns or restrictions you have, such as space limitations, etc. It's important to find the right fit. Ask how big the dog will be at age two. Staff may not know exactly, but one thing you can do is look at a young dog's (or puppy's) paws. Large paws suggest the dog will be large by age one or two. Puppies have a somewhat predictable growth timetable as long as the pet is packed up (more on that later) and not separated or isolated from its close caretakers.

Some dogs that end up in shelters may be riddled with fear and insecurity created by well-intentioned but inept humans who were unaware that a little knowledge and effort invested in their role as an alpha leader would have reaped great benefits for them and their canines. Rescues are looking for strong, demonstrative alphas to lead them to a secure promised land because, for whatever reason, the rescues have failed to pack up yet, and their very existence and survival depends on doing so.

What I discovered as a trainer is that most of the dogs that I'm called to work with are ten-to-twelve months old and going into the phase humans call the terrible twos. The common denominator among nearly all of them is that they lack previous training. It doesn't matter if they're from a shelter or a breeder—they come to me with bad habits. I motor through most of them rapidly because of my skill and experience, but as I do, it hits me that these owners could have saved a lot of trouble by starting the training of their dogs at a younger age.

I've also noticed a trend lately in my first-time sessions with new clients. Many of them believe that the training they did with their dog at a chain pet store class (using treat-based rewards) made their pet proficient in basic obedience. According to my evaluations, the dogs are not. Training with treat rewards may work for puppies or maturing beta dogs, and their owners, but alphas that slip through these programs are going to require praise and correction-based training as they approach twelve months of age.

So if you add a puppy to your family, I urge you to *get them to the vet* for a checkup and vaccination schedule and to *start their training as early as possible*—typically between four-to-six months of age. Find a reputable local trainer who can advise you at what age they will start working with your puppy. Don't wait—don't hem and haw—you'll regret it later.

And for those people who only yell at dogs, I suggest you purchase one of those fake parrots with recording devices that repeat your muttered curses back to you. You'll get what you give. Dogs are love, and we all grow and evolve into better people when we know and practice love.

PACK ANIMALS AND CRATE TRAINING

Repeat after me: Dogs are pack animals—they want *and need* to be part of a social clan. For domestic dogs, a pack is a group that offers comfort, security, and connection. Mental growth, confidence, maturity, and well-being can only happen when dogs are part of a pack, either with humans, dogs, or a combination thereof. If dogs aren't part of a pack, they'll be insecure, and that's the root of many behavior problems.

What constitutes a pack? When you bring a puppy or dog into your household, you and the inhabitants (human and other dogs) become their pack. At a minimum, the pack is you and your dog. If they can see, hear, and smell you, they're "packed up." This is essential to their growth and development. If left on their own, they don't learn or mature emotionally. That's why a large proportion of rescues often act much younger than their true age—because their development has been stunted by being separated or discarded from their pack.

Dogs should be a part of their group when possible, and that includes the overnight hours. They are terribly stressed when they aren't allowed to sleep in the den with their pack. Never isolate a puppy or dog in a separate location and all alone to sleep. No dog should be alone overnight, such as penned outside, shut in a laundry room, or put in the basement. It's cruel, and they won't learn anything good from it.

This doesn't mean that your dog must sleep in your bed. They can have their own dog crate in your bedroom and sleep there. They will be much more secure and less fearful. Once they are fully house-trained, you may let them sleep in your bed or on the bedroom floor if that's what you would like. But if you insist on having your dog sleep apart from you or other family members, then get another dog as a pack mate to sleep with it.

Consider crate training a must when bringing a pup into your household. Puppies need to spend as much time (often in a crate) with their pack so they can imprint the pack's activity and schedule. Instinctively, they'll attempt to mirror the behavior of the pack. This is one way they learn.

At night, puppies need to be crated at least until they are house-trained. It's essential for a puppy to develop muscles to hold off acts of elimination while in their sleeping spot. They don't like to soil where they sleep, so a perfectly sized crate is a place where a dog or pup will avoid peeing or pooping, provided that they aren't kept in there for too long.

A pup's crate should be just large enough for them to stand, sit, and turn around comfortably. Measure the dog's height and length then add five or six inches to each number, respectively—that's the size of the crate you should look for, no bigger. A crate that is too big gives the dog the sense that there's plenty of room in the crate for both sleeping and eliminating.

If you're unsure about the appropriate crate size, there are many online sources to help in the selection, including websites of pet product suppliers. You can also ask the staff at your local pet supply store how to pick the right size crate for your dog or pup. You may have to buy more crates as your puppy outgrows their current crate—how many different-sized crates you might need depends on how large the puppy will be when fully house-trained.

The rule of thumb for how long a puppy can stay in a crate is they can last one hour more than their age in months. Thus at three months old, a pup can last up to four hours in the crate.

If you don't crate the puppy overnight and have them in your bed with access to free roaming around the bedroom (or any other room), they'll wake up when they need to relieve themselves, walk a little way off, and pee. You'll be upset that they peed in your bed, bedroom, or inside the house, but the pup was doing what comes naturally.

For dogs that are not yet house-trained, crate training may work for them, too. After your dog or puppy has been crated for a while, have their leash ready before you release them from the crate. When you open the crate, be prepared to take them outside immediately. During the day, having their crate not too far from an outside door helps. With a puppy, just pick them up, clip on their leash, step outside, and set them down where you would generally like them to do their business.

When they've peed or pooped outdoors, praise them enthusiastically like, "Good pup. Good Max (or whatever their name). What a good, good, doggie!" This praise means so much to them and conditions them to repeat the behavior. *Do not* let them roam free in the house until they've done their business outside. Otherwise, they will pee or poo inside, which is what you're trying to avoid by using a crate.

Once they've eliminated outdoors, they can then be back inside the house, uncrated, for a while without you worrying about an accident. After some time, put them back in their crate and follow the rule of thumb on timing. Just before bedtime, take your puppy or untrained dog outside for a chance to eliminate and then crate them in your bedroom when the family sleeps.

When you crate your puppy at night, for the first week or two when they whimper, you can open the crate right away, pick them up, take them outside, and praise them when they do their business. At this early stage, they have little control. If you're a heavy sleeper and think you won't hear their whimpers, set an alarm for three-, four-, and five-month-old puppies at four, five, or six hours, respectively, after you crated them at bedtime. When your alarm signals, take them outside preemptively. Puppies grow fast, and the sooner you get started using crates, the sooner they'll gain control of their bathroom behavior.

Your puppy may soon outlast more than the calculated hours, but don't fault a puppy for an occasional accident. In the beginning, you'll encounter some mishaps where your pup pees or poos in the crate or in the house. Don't punish them because it only has a negative effect. Instead, stay calm and don't make a big fuss.

Given their incredible sense of smell, your puppy has already been subjected to enough distress sitting in their own stink. Take them outside or to the shower and clean them up. Clean their crate thoroughly and go on with your day. Turn obstacles into learning and create as much of a consistent routine as possible in their days so accidents rarely occur.

Keep the crate with your pack generally. Crate training may be easiest if you have two crates per puppy or dog—one in the main living area and one in the bedroom where you sleep. Most crates come with handles for carrying, so they can be moved around if necessary, and you may not want to purchase multiple crates until your puppy is at a size closer to what their full size will be.

A lot of my clients balked at crate training for one reason or another. Some people mistakenly consider it to be cruel, but they're thinking of humans, not dogs. To a dog, the right-sized crate is a cozy den. It's supposed to be their safe space, and you should treat it that way.

Dogs should feel secure in their crate. Teach all children and members of a household that when the dog or puppy is in the crate, they are not to be disturbed or bothered in any way. My younger sister's family had a Rhodesian ridgeback named Sydney. When the dog was full grown, they left her crate always open in the master bedroom walk-in closet. Sydney would get irritable in the evening and go upstairs into her crate. That was her sign for the humans to leave her alone. Well rested in the morning, Sydney would be her wonderful, easy-going self again.

At five or six weeks old, your puppy will have gotten all its baby teeth in. Baby teeth are razor-sharp, and between eight-and-sixteen weeks, those piranha teeth (as I call them) are constantly pushed from behind by adult teeth, causing the puppy pain and creating a desire to chew on the nearest object. I give them a Nylon chew in their crate in my presence or pet them next to me on a couch while holding the artificial bone so they can teethe. The more they chew, the faster the baby teeth will fall out, and the sooner the adult teeth will come in.

Not only does a crate help a puppy develop muscles to control their elimination but it also protects your dog from household dangers when you're away. And vice versa, with your pet crated while you're out of the house, your furniture, rugs, shoes, books, and so forth are safe from an anxious puppy scratching and chewing to relieve its stress while alone.

Choosing not to crate train your dog is detrimental to the whole training experience. As much as you love your dog, it's hard to exercise restraint when you come home to find a cherished heirloom or other valuable items destroyed. So prevent that from happening by using a crate until you know your dog can be trusted when you're out.

THE THREE TONES
OF TRAINING

A dog's supreme sense is that of smell which can be ten thousand to one hundred thousand times stronger than that of humans. Some experts say it's a million times stronger. The portion of a dog's brain that processes odors is much larger than that of the corresponding part in a human brain. Hearing—a dog's next strongest sense—is at least four times better than human hearing and covers a much wider range of frequencies.

Sight is the weakest of a dog's senses, but dogs are not totally color-blind. They see in muted shades and have better night vision than humans do. They also see movement keenly. Therefore, many dog trainers like to use moving hand signals in addition to verbal commands and whistles.

The abilities described above are generalizations— bear in mind that a particular dog's senses may vary by breed and individual. In cases where some breeds have been overbred without care about consequences, an individual dog may be deaf, blind, or both.

Fundamental in my work with dogs is conveying basic commands to them like an alpha trains their pack, that is, in a language dogs can understand with various postures and tones for what *is* and what *is not* acceptable in the pack. And remember, dogs are not multi-taskers: They can focus on only one thing at a time. They do not understand declarative and run-on sentences. Make every situation as black-and-white as you can for your four-legged buddy.

As I evolved as a trainer, I settled on a simple three-tone system of communicating information to the furry bundles of energy in my sessions. The three distinct verbal tones I use are command, correction, and praise.

The **command tone** uses a normal voice carried out in a firm, neutral, and monotonal manner. Issue a command once at normal speed, not too slow and not too fast. Give a pause of about three seconds to see if the dog responds.

The **correction tone** is short and sharp, delivered at a slightly raised volume. It gets a dog's attention but not in a pleasing way, like an abrupt *No* or *Nope!* Because dogs hear better than you do, there is no need to yell. Simply boost your voice a little. The correction tone breaks a dog's focus on unwanted behavior, but the tone should be used sparingly. For every correction tone I utter at an undesirable behavior, I give *many* more expressions of praise when a dog does something right.

The **praise tone** is higher pitched and delivered in a singsong style like baby talk. Use it immediately after a dog performs a command correctly or any time a dog displays a behavior you want to reinforce. In praise tone, my speech is faster and repetitive. I'm the gentleman you see walking dogs at a heel down the street vocalizing "good boy, good boy, good boy," or "good girl, good girl," etc.

If issued often and properly, praise tone encourages your dog to respond successfully to your commands because they would rather hear praise than corrections.

Using praise tone is silly, lighthearted fun. Just try to stay mad or resentful when going on and on in joyful tones. I can visit any dog I've trained and, using just my praise tone, get them wiggling on over to me. No matter the content, if praise tone is delivered in a loving tone, dogs love it. You could say "cootchy wootchy scootchy you're da worst dog I've ever known and if you chew anudder pair of my Air Jordans^{TM} I'm going to scream" in singsong praise talk, and your doggie would be wagging their ever-loving tail.

Of course, you wouldn't use the praise tone if you just caught your dog in the *act* of eating your shoes—that would be time for a correction tone No and for removing the leftovers as calmly as you could.

When your dog is fearful, don't coo or praise them; by doing so, you're rewarding them for undesirable behavior, and trust me, that's behavior you don't want. Instead of praising a dog who is scared, give them a command in your command tone to perform something that you know they can do, such as sit, stay, or come. This redirects your dog's attention to a specific task. When they accomplish it, then you reward them with your praise tone.

By responding to your command tone when afraid, the dog learns to deal with their fears and to trust that you, the alpha leader, will maintain pack security by handling any threats confronting the pack. With dogs, it's simple: You're the alpha and they look to you to take charge. If you don't, your dog could be overwhelmed by fear and stunted in their growth.

Practice using the different tones as you start to work with your dog on simple commands such as sit, stay, and come. It may feel unfamiliar at first, but with repetition, the learning process accelerates for both you and your dog. The more you use it, the easier it gets.

COLLARS AND TREATS

Two aspects of my dog training differ from those of current custom, namely the type of collars I like to use and employing only praise as a reward for desirable behavior.

When considering the collar you get for walking or training your dog, make sure it's snug enough that they can't back out of it when leashed. I prefer nylon slip collars and leads for most dogs. However, many people consider the use of slip collars and choke chain collars to be inhumane. This can be true if they are used incorrectly.

A choke collar is never meant to choke a dog. The choke collar's chain has a directionality and must be put on a dog's neck in a specific way. If the collar has been properly placed, a quick tug on the collar when a dog misbehaves creates a pinch followed by an immediate release. This is meant to get the attention of the dog and to interrupt an unwanted behavior. But if the chain has been put on the dog improperly, or if a handler constantly pulls on the leash, the constriction won't release, and thus the dog gets hurt.

If I'm working with large-breed, fearful, formerly abused rescues or dominant alpha males, I will occasionally use pinch or prong collars because they keep me from having to go pound-for-pound, muscle-to-muscle with those dogs. I need to conserve my strength and endurance when trying to help a dog that could present a physical challenge to me. I'm versed in correct placement and careful use of those collars.

If you choose to use nylon or chain slip collars, please get educated on how to put on and use those collars correctly. Helpful videos can be found online by searching for "how to use a slip collar correctly" in your web browser's search bar, and only view videos made by professional dog trainers. A local trainer or staff at a dog training or boarding facility should also be able to show you how to do this or suggest an alternative option—such as a martingale collar—that will work for training and walking your dog.

A martingale collar combines a regular buckle collar with a slip collar and gives you more control without tightening past a fixed amount. Because of this limited slip, there is less chance it could hurt your dog. The martingale collar has two loops: one that you size snugly to your dog's neck by adjusting it so you can fit two fingers under the strap; and another loop that, when attached to a leash and pulled, will exert some tension on the other loop but will not choke the dog.

If you choose to use a martingale collar, learn how to fit the collar properly and note that the collars are designed for training and walking *only when leashed*. They should not be left on an unattended or unleashed dog because the loop part that attaches to the leash can hang down and get caught on a fence or other object.

As for rewarding a dog when they perform a welcome behavior, I only use praise and petting. These days, many folks offer a small treat as a reward. I prefer not using treats when training because I'm old-school, and treat-rewarded dogs tend to beg when you're having meals or a party at your house. By the way, it's important to tell your guests that they should *not* feed your dog party food. Certain foods are bad for dogs and can make them sick, plus some dogs have food allergies.

Only reward a dog for behavior you want. Do not reward a dog for begging by giving them food, or you are conditioning them to keep begging. It may seem cute at first, but it's soon an annoyance that won't go away.

There are many online training videos teaching a variety of ways to train a dog—using treats, dog toys, or praise with no treats. Praise doesn't cost you a thing, and you don't need to buy a pouch for your belt to put it in. It's up to you, but the important point about training is that it should *never* involve yelling or punishment.

Don't ever hit or kick your dog because it will eventually bite you or somebody else. Don't scream at, yell at, or chase your dog, because cornered, fearful animals are the most dangerous animals on the planet. And never correct for anything after-the-fact—dogs live in the immediate moment. Training a dog is all about patience, practice, and positivity. Praise everything they do right. Dogs soak that up!

TRAINING BASICS

There is an oft quoted maxim attributed to various athletes: The more I practice, the luckier I get. Funny how that works. The hardest part of getting a dog on track when it comes to behavior is owner participation and compliance with training protocol.

If you acquire a puppy and take the time to train, exercise, walk daily or near daily, and reward them with praise and affection, you'll have a companion who will follow you to the gates of hell and back. That should be your goal.

And the training part of the equation doesn't have to go on forever. Dogs can be taught all they need to know to be a good pack member in a relatively short time if you're consistent.

If you aren't an active registered breeder, neuter or spay your puppies before they're a year old. The testosterone levels in males decrease significantly in the weeks after being neutered, which also helps greatly with house training. With less testosterone, neutered males don't have as strong an urge to frequently mark territory, and they're less likely to become aggressive dogs.

There's a myth about how spaying a female dog too early can negatively impact their health—I've found it to be untrue. The female dogs I've owned were spayed around eight months of age, and their health and maturation were not hampered in the least. Talk to your veterinarian if you're unsure on this matter.

When your dog is young, get them used to your touch. Groom them with your hands at first, then progress to using a comb or brush. They should look forward to your touch, not shrink from it. After your puppy has received its recommended shots, you can walk them and start their training.

If your dog has lots of energy, consider playing with them or walking them (if they're manageable on leash) before a training session to release some of their vigor. Most dogs take immediately to walking, but others need encouragement. In that case, I'll just walk with a dog short-leashed at my side while saying heel and muttering good dog for any movement they make with me. Then I stop, help them find the sit position, and pour on the praise and petting.

As long as you don't exhaust your dog, they'll do better with training if they've gotten some exercise before you start.

Bring a good mood to your practice sessions. It's important to refrain from showing frustration or losing your temper. If you have low blood sugar, eat a healthy snack. If you're in a bad mood, train at another time. Some humans in a hurry get impatient and give up, claiming their dog is stupid. Wolves and dogs are not stupid.

Recall the three distinctly different verbal tones described in the preceding chapter—**command** (regular voice, clear, and calm), **correction** (sharp and succinct), and **praise** (singsong happy). Employ these tones to teach your dog the basic commands sit, stay, come, down, and down-stay.

Start training with your dog on a leash that is three-to-six feet long. Do this in your yard, a room in your house if there is sufficient space, or a quiet corner in a park without distractions. Any time your dog does what you're commanding, reward them immediately with praise and petting.

For sit training, while your dog is standing, take a position at their side near their head and shoulders. In command tone, say Sit and touch their hind end with gentle pressure. Do *not* push or force their rear end down. If they sit, praise them with enthusiasm. Soon they should sit on command without any touch. As your dog masters sit, you can move around to their front and practice a few times from that position.

For stay, while your dog is sitting, hold the leash above your dog's head (not too tightly), issue the command Stay, touch the top of their head and walk around them. Stay close—no further than three feet away—as you circle them. While you're working close to your dog, watch them for fear tells such as ears back, tail tucked, and flinches when your feet are near your dog's rear end. Be calm and praise them constantly if they stay in place.

If your dog moves out of the stay, give a quick short tug on the leash while saying a brief, sharp No or Hey. When the dog stops moving, instantly praise them in a loving tone and try again. As you experience success, gradually increase how far you are from the dog when you walk around them. Ultimately, you'll get out to six-foot circles if your leash is that long.

Once you've succeeded with stay, face your dog head-on and back up about three to six feet. Squat or go down on one knee and call your dog with either their name or the command Come. The lower you can get your body for this exercise, the easier it is for the dog to approach and sit instead of jumping up on you. Staying low also concentrates your scent and pheromones right there in front of your pooch. Dogs live for your smells!

As an aside, jumping up and pushing on people is an unwelcome behavior that you don't want to reward, especially in large dogs. A lot of healthy young people I've worked with want their dog to stand on their hind legs and hug them, but the behavior can come back to bite them in the tushy (figuratively) when their older parents or grandparents get "hugged" too roughly or a little kid gets knocked over accidentally. Tots and older folks can easily be toppled, and if they fall over and hit something hard, it can have serious consequences. So don't praise your dog if they jump up on you or anyone.

Back to training: If your dog doesn't come when called, repeat the command and give a gentle tug on their leash. If they come to you, reward them with a cheery voice then help them find the sit position by touching down on their bottom while saying Sit. When your dog sits, praise profusely with petting and the praise tone.

With enough practice and reinforcement, your dog will eventually master the come command, and you won't have to do it in a low position anymore. You'll be able to stand and say Come, and your dog will come without jumping on you.

Another option one can add in training is the use of a hand or arm signal when issuing a vocal command. For example, when I call a dog to come, I extend my right arm straight out to the side then bring it in to my chest. The movement in the signal is important because it's the motion that the dog's eyesight discerns.

Hand signals are useful in the case when your dog is off-leash, and the wind is blowing from behind them so they can't hear you well. Remember, though, that your dog should never be off-leash unless they're in an area that is appropriately safe and designated as an off-leash area, and unless your dog is well trained. Traffic is a great danger to off-leash dogs.

For heel, use a short leash and start with your dog in sit position by your side. Command Heel and walk forward encouraging your dog to join you. Hold the shortened leash out to the side to discourage your dog from going ahead of you. If your dog moves ahead of you, correct with No, then stop and start over with your dog by your side.

Remember, you are the alpha of your pack so you must lead. If your dog leads, they will assume the alpha position and you don't want that. Any time your dog stays walking by your side for a few steps, praise them.

To teach down and down-stay, start with your dog in the sit position. Get on one knee beside them near their head. Command Down while touching them on their shoulder with slight, downward pressure of your arm. At the same time, pat the ground in front of them with the hand of your other arm. *Do not force* them down.

Don't be concerned with form initially because it's a process that takes time. The down position is the most vulnerable one for a dog to perform. When going into this position, a beta dog might roll onto their side to offer submission, and that's okay. An alpha might just bounce right back up, but be patient, back off, call them to you, repeat the command, and praise the dog when they go down.

For down-stay, once the dog is in the down position, hold their leash up (without tugging) and walk around them, commanding Stay. If they stay down, praise them and repeat Stay as you continue circling them. If they succeed, you can try walking around them a little further away.

While teaching your dog or puppy this sequence of commands, keep in mind the abilities and physical development of your individual pet. When your puppy goes through a growth spurt, they may have trouble focusing on commands. This is understandable. For some puppies I've boarded and trained, it's as though they went to bed driving a MINI Cooper but woke up behind the wheel of a full-sized Chevy Silverado. They have a hard time controlling their own body and don't even know what's going on.

Be patient. You don't have to accomplish it all at once. While working with your dog, observe their individual limits and comfort zones. Don't force them beyond such bounds.

If you or your dog are tired or losing attention, take a break after you have some success with one or two commands, then continue training at another time that works. Practice *success*, not failure, and try to finish each session on a high note.

When your dog can perform sit, stay, and come five times in a row on a leash six feet away from you, you've achieved a lot! You're ready for the next step: Drop the leash—if you're in a safe enclosed area—and practice the commands anew. See if your dog will perform without you holding their leash. If they're not up to it yet, just backtrack a little by picking up the leash and starting over with sit.

When your dog can complete the basic commands with their leash dropped, try giving the commands further away from them, and gradually increase the distance if your dog succeeds.

Think about your tones while observing your dog. Are you overcorrecting them or starting to lose your temper? This is common if you feel overwhelmed. When you are about to lose it (or have already lost it), recenter yourself by taking some deep breaths. Once calm, call your dog to and lavish praise on them with their first step toward you.

If your dog doesn't come to you and the training session has broken down, lie down and whimper like a lost, hurt animal. If you've created any bond with your puppy or dog, they will come to investigate. Praise them when they do.

One of the many gifts of dogs is their uncanny capacity to forgive the impatient, frustrated humans who have subjected them to too much correction. Tomorrow is another day for patience, persistence, and praise to help you and your dog become fluid partners. When that happens, you'll feel like you've won the sparkling Mirror Ball Trophy on *Dancing with the Stars*.

COVERING GROUND ON THE DAILY WOLF PACK WALK

I can't overemphasize the importance of daily power walks for your dog. I'm adamant about it because there's a big payoff—better behavior and increased bonding with your dog. Dogs have an innate drive to walk daily. It re-creates their wolf ancestors' daily hunts for food. Dogs love to cover ground, mark turf, and sniff out and reply to pee-mail left by other dogs. Ever since I started training dogs in 1971 while serving in the US Army, I've included covering ground in my method of nurturing the magnificent creation of a finely tuned pack.

It's good for us humans to get some fresh air and exercise too. I've trained folks with paraplegia and quadriplegia plus older adults in wheelchairs, motorized chairs, scooters, and even golf carts how to walk their dogs as often as they are able. It burns off a canine's excess energy thus helping them to chill out.

On your walks, be attentive. If you're distracted by your phone, you won't be able to observe your dog and keep on top of things. Carry your phone in a pocket, waist pack, or belt bag. As the alpha leader, you should be aware of your surroundings.

At Bad Dogs, we started every day with a hike at an area park. Simulating a wolf pack hunt in which the wolves don't eat until after they've caught prey, I didn't feed my dogs or the boarders their morning allotment of food until we returned from our walk. In response, my boarding dogs packed up and worked as a team faster.

Don't free-feed your dog unless you've consulted your veterinarian and they've recommended it for specific reasons. Find the total amount of food your dog requires daily by using the information (usually dog weight and age) printed on the dog food bag, then divide that amount by two and feed your dog that quantity twice daily (once in the morning and once at dinner time).

If your dog is exercised a lot, you may be able to give them a bit more than the recommended amount. Ask your vet if you're not sure how much your dog should eat.

On the hikes with Midnight at my heels, I realized the power of the pack to act as one entity, a team that imparted confidence to those who needed it. Dogs that boarded with us became socialized with our pack, and the daily hike was good for them. An exception was made for puppies or dogs that weren't ready or able to walk far. Puppies can't take long hikes at first, but between four-to-six months old, they can begin with shorter walks and build up their endurance over time.

Puppies experience growth spurts just like human kids do, so daily exercise to develop muscles that support bone growth is essential. At Bad Dogs, I walked puppies separately in the neighborhood then crated them in the house before loading up the rest of the pack for the drive to the park.

If your dog gets nervous or nauseous in cars, practice sit, down, and down-stay obedience in the car while stationary. And remember, *never leave a dog in a car on a hot day* unless you are with them *and* the air conditioner is on. To train the dog, reassure and praise them if they stay calm. After success with that, try driving on short trips with your dog. Reassure them in the car with lots of cheery praise and take them to places other than the veterinarian's office.

Over time, I lengthened the walking distance for newbie walkers according to their ability and stamina. Some dogs resisted walks at first, but they usually came around to liking it. As we covered ground, I praised them constantly. Younger dogs watched older, well-trained, off-leash dogs respond to my verbal commands and receive praise. The youngsters naturally started mirroring the behavior and wanting that praise too.

Most dogs can't help but get in the groove because their need to pack up is essential and ingrained. When this happens, your pack functions like a well-oiled machine—it's a fascinating process to be a part of.

When going for a walk, know your environment and the weather for the day and time. Be prepared—I pack plenty of water for all the doggies and a collapsible bowl in which to dispense it.

Dogs perspire through their tongues. You can tell if a dog is dehydrated by touching their tongue with your hand. If their tongue is dry, provide water immediately. If your dog limps, check the pads on their paws with your hands. There may be a small pebble, burr, or bit of other plant material stuck in their pads that you can remove.

Buy a roll of poop bags and carry at least two or three bags with you. Please clean up after your pet—it's the right thing to do, and you set an example when people see you doing it. Though your dog will need to pee or poop, and want to sniff everything along the way, try to limit frequent stopping, especially after they've done their business. I don't dawdle or let my protégés investigate every bush, pole, mailbox, and fire hydrant. I prefer to power walk them at a heel.

The objective is to establish a consistent pace together, and typically that should settle in within a quarter to a half mile. If you stroll in a stop-go-stop-go fashion the entire time, it's much harder to get into the rhythm of a productive walk. Covering ground as steadily as you can is what an alpha does. This reassures the pack because they benefit from a top dog who leads them, burns off their excess energy, and doesn't give them time to be afraid.

If other people with dogs approach while you're walking with your dog, step to the side of the trail or sidewalk, if possible, and issue Sit and Stay commands to your dog. Then stand close or slightly over them while the "threatening pack" cruises past.

This focuses your dog's attention on *you* rather than on the party passing by. Here you demonstrate that you're the alpha of your pack, and thus your dog feels secure knowing you will protect them. For their pack, a demonstrative alpha eliminates the gray areas and makes everything black-and-white.

If your dog gets away from you and takes off running, you may naturally start chasing after them. Resist this urge to chase. Dogs have four legs while you have only two—who do you think is going to win? And given that dogs *love* the chase game, you'll be at it for a while wasting your time and energy.

Instead of pursuing your dog, choose to step up and act like an alpha leader. You have an advantage: Your dog doesn't really like being separated from you. You offer the company and security of the pack, so if your dog wanders or runs off, stand still and call them lovingly. If they stop, *praise* them. If they make some steps back toward you, *praise* them.

Make them want to come back to you. If you stand there, yell, and swear, "G**dammit, come," they are not going to come—unless they're masochistic (which dogs aren't)—because your tone telegraphs to them you're going to punish them upon arrival.

If your dog keeps moving away from you, stay calm, walk backward slowly, and continue to call their name in a pleasant manner. They should soon feel the mental tug of the bond you've created with them. The pull of the pack is powerful. For dogs it means not only comfort but survival as well.

Such a bond is generally unbreakable, unless a dog's prey drive has kicked in. This happens with hunting dogs who pick up a scent trail or with sight hounds who see moving prey such as rabbits or squirrels. Once they're overcome by this tunnel vision, it may be a while before their concentration on the prey is broken and they come back to you.

Bear in mind, your dog is dependent on you when it's packed up. That's why your aim is to be a responsible, reliable pack leader—fulfilling your dog's needs without spoiling them, and teaching them good behavior with rewards instead of punishment. In this way, your dog will want to please you and usually won't be comfortable straying too far.

When coming home from work or an outing, don't pick your dog up or put it on your lap and pet it—this sends the wrong message that your dog is the alpha of your pack. Allowing your dog to be the alpha of the house is not love—it's a recipe for an unhappy, ineffective, and insecure pack that doesn't interact safely with non-pack humans and dogs. Certainly you can pet and hug your dog, but put it on the chair or sofa *beside* you, not on top of you.

Consistently walking and practicing with your pet as much as you can—preferably daily—will bond you with your pet like you wouldn't believe. You'll tap into your dog's working ability, experience endorphins, stay fit, and fashion a lifelong personal trainer who only bills you for love and affection. After morning walks, you'll face the day energized, centered, and prepared to deal with life's ups and downs with all your faculties engaged.

Upon returning with Midnight, Aiko, and our boarders from a morning Bad Dogs hike, I would pull into the garage, close the door, and herd the well-exercised, content dogs into the house and feed them. With their stomachs full and stores of energy dissipated, the dogs settled down easily, ready for naps.

There are even more benefits to engaging as an alpha leader in walks with your dog. You learn to anticipate and prevent problems before they escalate, and you and your dog coalesce into a pack—it brings you both boundless joy.

The daily walks, training my dogs using the various tones, and praising them for every pleasing and cooperative behavior has given me something I can only describe as a sixth sense, though sometimes it feels more like a superpower.

NOTES ON AGGRESSION

There are three distinct kinds of aggression in dogs: Fear aggression is exhibited by a tucked tail, barking and backing up, crouching, snarling, and baring teeth with ears back and flat; dominance aggression is marked by a straight-up tail, chest puffed out, head up, plus barking and lunging forward; and seizure-related aggression is when a dog snaps for no apparent reason, and its eyes go blank or have a distant stare. Signals in the synapses of the dog's brain are misfiring.

To avoid getting bitten when any of these aggressions are displayed, it's best to relax and give the dog some space. Dogs with fear aggression, also referred to as fear biters, will wildly strike at anyone approaching in a threatening or pushy manner, especially if cornered.

Facing a dog with this reaction, often a rescue or puppy that has been beaten or hit, one must stand still, relax, and praise the dog.

Yelling and screaming elevates the dog's perception of threat and will increase their aggression. Conversely, remaining still and quiet relieves the dog's distress and agitation, so it will begin to calm. As the dog relaxes, people can slowly back away. Eventually regaining its normal composure, the dog should come if praised lavishly and if there's no tension or anger expressed in the dog's presence.

A person who has anger issues and poor self-control would be a terrible match as the owner of a dog with fear aggression (or maybe any dog for that matter).

To get over crippling fear, an abused dog must learn to interpret human actions in a new light. After establishing trust with such a dog, I introduce hand and foot positions that simulate hitting or kicking—but in slow motion and never connecting. From above the dog's head, I bring a hand downward as though I'm going to hit them, but all the time I'm praising. When they flinch, it's clear they've been hit in the past. I back off, continue the praise, and stroke them slowly.

I do the same with my foot, making a slow motion as if I'm going to kick them, but I praise them and stop the advancing foot when they react to it. In this way, they relearn that the hand and foot are not threatening. This process must be repeated many times. I start slowly, and then in successive sessions as a dog gets more comfortable with my movements, I incrementally speed up the motion.

In cases of dominance aggression, such as when a dog is protecting its family or property, a dog might seize my arm, hand, or anything they can get a good grip on. I just relax and don't pull away or offer resistance. I tell the family members to back away from me and the dog. This almost always defuses the situation.

When I'm severely attacked while training a dog, I lift the leash and collar straight up over the dog's head, tautly, to temporarily disarm it. This takes a quick and strong action on my part. I try to prevent these situations, but sometimes they happen.

When it comes to seizure-related aggression, in my experience, it's hard to diagnose. If there are no flags or triggers causing the aggression, chances are it will be difficult, if not impossible, to predict and manage incidents—nor will training fix it.

The next step would be to see a reputable veterinarian about how to proceed. If there's no resolvable physical issue, seizure-related aggressive dogs are dangerous and not remediable. My recommendation in such cases is to have them euthanized because it's a poor quality of life for the dog and the owner.

In the late 1990s, I was the cleanup hitter in the big leagues of dog training for aggressive dogs in Arizona. If a dog bit someone and it was reported, either the owner of the dog or the state quarantined the dog for fourteen days while it was checked for rabies. After the dog was released from quarantine, if the dog bit another person, it would most likely be euthanized, especially if the dog showed a pattern of aggression. There were possible exceptions to euthanasia if it could be shown that the person who was bitten, or the people around that person, had provoked the dog to attack.

Owners who had never gotten on top of the situation for one reason or another would call all the trainers listed in the phone book to see who could help them before their dog went on record for a second bite. Most trainers didn't work with aggressive dogs, but believing my main purpose on earth was to help dogs coexist with humans, I always offered to give the dog of a distressed owner a chance.

One family I worked with had a gaggle of active young boys and a rescued border collie that nipped. I observed the dog with the parents and the boys. The dog responded to the parents adequately but not so much to the kids. If the situation got frantic, the dog started darting around and the potential for the boys to be hurt increased amid the chaos.

If someone raised their voice at the dog, he started nipping. To prevent the escalation to full-blown biting, the nipped victim had to freeze, and the dog would back off and calm down. Once he calmed down, you could leash him and relocate him to a quieter locale. After much work, the parents thanked me, and hopefully they altered their behavior enough to overcome this dog being put in overstimulating situations.

Another case I worked on was a Maltese-minipoodle mix named Max who was rescued by a lovely older couple. Max became aggressive at the drop of a hat for no apparent reason. After working with him for a while, I diagnosed him with a rare form of seizure-related aggression. When his brain chemistry got out of whack, the wrong messages were fired between his synapses, resulting in aggression. If you were highly observant, you could see it coming on and crate him. The alternative was to load him up on medication which I didn't recommend because he weighed under ten pounds and the desired dosage was hard to control.

One of the most aggressive dogs I ever worked with was an unneutered sixty-pound chow. A veterinarian had handed his owners my business card after his arm was freed from the jaws of their dog (thanks to an alert vet tech who had quickly tranquilized the offending biter).

This chow was dominant aggressive and attempted to bite me several times during our first session, but I avoided getting bitten by being observant and responding quickly with dominating tactics. The dog came around to training rather well. I then had the couple's teenage boy practice with him successfully. I scheduled the second session for the following week and advised the kid to work with him daily and avoid conflicts.

The family canceled the second appointment but had me out several weeks later. When I arrived, the teen handed me the leash with the chow at the end of it. With immediate recognition and resolve, the dog launched at me and locked his powerful jaws around my left thigh. Obviously he favored dark meat.

Having experience with aggressive dogs before, I tugged the leash and issued a sharp No. His fury increased, and he bit down harder. Everything slowed and became quite clear.

Focusing my energy, I reached under his head with my right hand and clenched his throat where his artery and windpipe ran. Shortly after, he gasped for air, releasing his excruciating, viselike grip on my flesh. I calmly returned him to his owners, informing them that the dog would have to be euthanized. Unfortunately, there was nothing we could do because that chow was blooded and therefore irretrievable.

As I later sat on a surgical table at the VA hospital having my wound cleansed and dressed and feeling the effects of a pain-killing shot, I pondered the old adage: humans get angry, dogs go mad.

If a dog goes mad, bites you or your dog, and won't let go, it's important not to panic. As hard as it is to stay calm, any resisting, kicking, or punching escalates the situation. Instead, just freeze. See if the biter then releases its hold. If they keep a firm lock on you or your pet, and there is no one around who can call for emergency help, reach under the dog's jaw, grab its throat, and squeeze until it lets go.

By shutting down the flow of blood and oxygen to its brain and lungs, you'll reset their emotional state back to non-aggression. It may seem like irrelevant babble, but if you ever find yourself in that situation, it just might save you or your pet.

And if you're blessed like me, you may find yourself having a carefree medication-induced moment while waiting for your ride to pick you up and ferry you home from the hospital.

Part III

A SUBLIME DANCE

N ow that I've covered some fundamentals of responsible and effective dog care and have offered the promise—with patience and consistent work—of developing an immensely rewarding relationship between a dog and their people, this last section of the book relates a few stories showcasing some of the colorful characters I've worked with throughout my career.

Concerning dog owners who sought my services, in our first sessions I asked lots of questions while trying my best to avoid putting them on the defensive. Many people were interested in learning more about their dynamic with their dog and how we could work to condition good interactions and behavior.

Sometimes I encountered couples—let's call them the "Bickersons"—who adamantly disagreed with each other about what rules and approaches should be operative in their home and for training their dog. If drama and discord dominated the initial session, I realized the owners needed a marriage counselor or divorce lawyer more than they needed me. In those cases, I gave the Bickersons exercises to practice individually with their dog and wished them well.

For other clients who saw the potential in my method of reinforcing with praise, I offered a flexible program of eight-to-twelve sessions, typically two per week for either four or six weeks, a package that came with satisfaction guaranteed or their money back. Initial sessions were conducted in their homes to master the basics (sit, stay, and come) with no distractions. Then we would venture outside for a few sessions to learn and practice heel on walks.

I fell in love with all the dogs. Their loving natures inspired me to do better every day. With my clients, I tried to create a genial atmosphere and a lively, but not rushed, tempo that enabled them to get into a good zone when working with their pets.

I guided them in becoming communicative, loving alpha leaders of their pack. It was a challenge for some clients to understand that it's best for everyone, including their dog, if the owner behaves like the master and leader of the pack instead of acting like their dog is a spoiled human child who calls all the shots.

When owners practiced the exercises I gave them, it showed at their next appointment. Clients exhibited more confidence, and their dogs got into the zone quickly. Seeing their progress, folks were more apt to stick with the program.

I paid attention to an owner's behavior as well as to that of their dog. When clients were oblivious or frozen with fear, I interjected with humor and lighthearted theatrics to march them right up to the boundary of a new goal and cross it without getting stuck in discouragement or overanalysis.

Creating positive patterns and behaviors to replace negative habits, I only had roughly a month to do so for many clients. I adjusted my style to keep them engaged and receptive, and reminded couples not to criticize each other's work, because they weren't going to do things exactly the same—yet they would reach the same goals.

When people are open to the training process, it works like a miracle. It's a sublime dance that engages dogs and owners together: Love, praise, and positive communication grow while fear, worry, and punishment fade.

This overview of my training experience is somewhat simplified because every human and dog are different, behaving with their own distinct personalities and idiosyncrasies. But it's wonderful to work successfully with clients and their dogs, because once canines are in their pack with a comfortable place in the pack order, the family environment is enhanced many times over.

BELLA OF THE BALL

Arriving at a quaint property nestled on a cul-de-sac in Phoenix's Pointe Resort, I rang the doorbell. A high-pitched puppy bark greeted me, further alerting the homeowners to my appearance. An amiable couple welcomed me inside and introduced me to Bella, an adorable wheaten terrier puppy who danced around and intently sniffed my clothing. I was sure she got a good whiff of my pack. Bella smiled and cavorted, batting her Tammy Faye eyelashes at me.

From Sydney, Australia, Bella's owners were in the US to run the public relations and marketing for an author tour. They informed me they had purchased Bella from a pet store at a local mall, and she was now seven months old. They wanted to get her started on basic obedience. It didn't take long to figure out why.

Bella was an alpha female wrapped in a perpetual-motion puppy torso. To label the dog a whirling dervish of pleasant pulchritude would be an understatement. The woman admitted that Bella wouldn't come or stay and often scared visitors who came to the house. But they'd been successful at crate training, so I congratulated them on that.

The terrier group is made up of breeds that are spirited, strong-minded dogs with intense prey drives. They do best with firm, steady owners. It would take some diligence to get Bella to pay attention to me and accept my praise, command, and correction tones. The dog could become an excellent companion, security system, and even a service dog of sorts to enhance her owners' golden years. But it would require that her subservient owners commit to learn my program and practice putting her through her paces.

If they didn't get on top of the situation, Bella would grow into an adult terrier who ruled their lives with erratic behavior. And when visitors entered the house, all it would take for the situation to go south with this gorgeous alpha was for someone to be frightened by the barking, exuberant, domineering dog. Imagine guests attempting to push Bella away with their hands—she might react by biting. These thoughts tugged on my heartstrings because it would be a tragedy all around.

I eased a slip collar over Bella's head past champagne-colored ringlets of hypoallergenic hair and leashed her. She winked at me as if to say *let the games begin*. When I started with my usual fundamentals of sit and stay, she displayed her contempt for the leash by performing exquisite alligator rolls, standing on her hind legs, and grabbing the leash with her front paws.

Given this was my first time working with her, instead of a brief tug on her lead and a sharp, correction tone No, I went back through the routine until Bella became mesmerized by the praise. I eventually got her to do a short sit and stay after a few corrections, and she then responded to Come with me kneeling and luring her in with "good girl, good girl, good girl."

Bella was whip-smart, and her owners were pushovers wrapped around her little paws. I recommended to the couple that they use a small nylon slip collar on her, demonstrating a few simple exercises for them to practice with Bella daily. But her owners mistakenly felt that for them to take the alpha role over Bella meant they didn't love her or that love was not a priority. They thought the way to show love was to spoil their pet in every way.

Keep in mind, dogs are descended from wolves, not teddy bears sold at Disneyland. To be the alpha leader in your home doesn't take anything away from the love you feel for your dog. Of course you love your dog! Taking charge while rewarding your pet for *good* behavior consistently helps your dog feel calm and secure.

Returning a week later for the next session, I introduced the down command to Bella's repertoire. She defied me like a toddler resisting having their face washed. I knew that getting Bella to relinquish control on her turf, where her human parents catered to her every whim, was going to be a challenge.

The couple traveled frequently for their work and inquired if I could board Bella while they were away. This was fortuitous, a chance to get Bella embedded with my pack on my turf. Her resistance would be futile, and her training could evolve quickly and naturally.

The day I brought her home for a stay at Bad Dogs, she greeted my pack with puppy glee and submission. Midnight and Aiko responded with typical adult dog indifference. I had a two-week window of opportunity to turn things around, which I jumped on. At the crack of dawn the next morning, we hiked in the desert with my dogs off-leash and Bella leashed at a reluctant heel.

After the excursion, I crated Bella and told my dogs to down-stay. They did, and Bella soon mirrored their down-stay in her crate. After returning from several other jobs a few hours later, I released her from the crate. A little later, I walked into the backyard. By way of the dog door, Midnight and Aiko joined me in the yard. Bella followed right behind them.

My dogs knew the drill and relieved themselves. Bella took a pee shortly after. As I brushed and groomed my dogs, Bella got in line for her turn. She emulated the pack like an understudy for the lead in a Broadway play.

As the training continued, I added a pinch collar to make resisting the down command unpleasant. I doubled the praise because I knew once her owners got back and Bella went home, she might revert to the princess status they had bestowed upon her. She would be back in the alpha position ruling the roost.

When Bella's stay at my place was over, I delivered her back to her bucolic little home. She pranced and licked her owners' faces while their joy upon being reunited with her almost overcame their jet-lagged weary bodies. I scooted out of there to leave them to their reunion.

At their next session, it was obvious the terrier would never make progress unless her owners were more consistent and resolute with her. I assessed those chances as slim to none. Bella was the apple of their eyes. But once again the universe smiled on me, and they made reservations for her next boarding while they traveled the US promoting their client and his book.

Bella touched me in many ways, and she eventually became as responsive off-leash as my own dogs. When staying with us, she was allowed on the couch and would assume a bit of a dominant spot up there on occasion. If I admonished other puppies for mis-behaving, she would fly off the sofa like lightning to get them in line. Yet once the moment had passed, she would sidle back to me and touch my soul with one glance from her large brown eyes fringed in warm halos.

She was a love! In due course, she mastered basic obedience and needed no more training, but I boarded her from time to time. It never ceased to amaze me how, in the middle of chasing a jackrabbit, she would turn on a dime when I called her and fly back to my side to hear "good girl, good girl, good girl."

Eventually the couple, with Bella in tow, moved back to Australia. I remember her fondly. Bella will always be in my heart, and if you'd met her, she would have wiggled her way into your heart, too, in a matter of minutes.

JASPER AND THE ELVIS LIP

I boarded a dog named Jasper, a scruffy, alpha-male schnauzer-mix weighing in at twenty pounds and standing not quite two feet tall. The bluff and bluster he exhibited were unbelievable. On one occasion when Jasper was boarding at Bad Dogs, I gave Midnight, Aiko, and Jasper each a bone and stepped out to make a phone call. When I returned ten minutes later, Jasper lay on all three bones while Midnight and Aiko, both larger than Jasper, stood boneless, docile, and flummoxed.

Jasper loved walking with our pack. He taught Midnight and Aiko much about posturing to influence the younger pack members. When the energetic roughhousing of puppies got too chaotic, Jasper froze them in their tracks with the Elvis Lip, where he'd softly snarl and quiver his upper lip. Aiko was riveted by his display.

Though he never challenged me, Jasper could swagger and project his dominance better than any dog his size I ever met. He brought great conviction and focus to his posturing, selling his lip routine so well that he never needed to follow up with aggressive action. With just a cock of his head, his lip quiver, and the metronomic swing of his erect tail, Jasper flustered and disarmed big dogs and puppies into submission. They would all back off and chill out as if hypnotized.

I loved that little guy for all that he showed us about confidence and how to carry oneself. He had the heart of a lion and the fortitude of an alpha wolf pack leader. Mirroring Jasper's behavior, Midnight and Aiko learned to control the puppies with just a muzzle and an upright tail. From then on, any time Jasper came to board at Bad Dogs, other dogs and puppies in our pack du jour faced a triple threat. None would challenge the trio of invincible Elvis Lips.

SWEET TALL FIERCE SIERRA

Sierra was fifteen weeks old when I arrived on the scene. The family that hired me to train her had no idea what breed she was when they purchased her. It turned out that this canine angel, a gorgeous, lanky cream-colored puppy with a charcoal muzzle, was an Anatolian shepherd. With her bright dark eyes and matching black eyelashes, she captured my heart.

Anatolian shepherds are smart working dogs from Turkey, initially bred to guard flocks of sheep and goats. The breed is used at ranches in the greater Phoenix area to protect livestock such as llamas and ostriches from coyotes and other predators.

Though fierce with predators, the large and powerful Anatolians are incredibly gentle with children and livestock. Strongly territorial, their downside is the ruckus they make when strangers or intruders appear near their turf, which is why it can be difficult to keep Anatolians in suburban neighborhoods.

Sierra was a gawky pup who trained easily but needed considerable daily exercise to help limit the energy she held in reserve for hypervigilance and vocalization when she perceived neighbors in their own backyards as encroaching on her family's turf.

In Sierra's household, the husband went to work early and came home late, and his wife had her hands full raising a four-year-old child and taking care of the home. Understandably, it was a challenge for the couple to find time to exercise the dog.

After six weeks of training, the clever Sierra had mastered basic obedience and our sessions ended. But her barking in territorial defense of the family home did not abate, and not long after, the couple called and asked if I would take her off their hands. I did gladly. Sierra immediately packed up with Midnight and Aiko. The three of them were agreeable and communicated well. On our morning hikes in the desert, I couldn't let her off-leash because of her inbred attention to animals outside of her pack.

I immediately started looking for another family to place her with because she would soon outgrow my dogs, and I didn't want her taking Midnight's position as queen of the pack. The longer Sierra stayed with us, the harder it would be for her to bond with another new pack.

Finally locating a lovely family with a two-acre horse property—minus the horses—and interested in taking her, I worked with them to understand the challenges associated with Anatolians. They soon fell madly in love with her, and shortly after, acquired a large golden retriever puppy named Rocky for her to pack up with.

I stayed in touch with them, and they told me that Sierra had an intense, authoritative bark on their property, but it was manageable by providing her with exercise and companionship that were so essential to her well-being.

I boarded Sierra from time to time when they traveled, and she never once challenged Midnight or Aiko, even though Sierra could have whipped them both with one paw tied behind her back.

Whenever she arrived for a stay, our dogs would greet her like a long-lost daughter. Sierra adjusted her behavior to fit in, though I could tell she missed her own family. Thankfully, because she wasn't on her home turf, she dialed back her barking when she stayed with us.

Sierra lived to be fifteen years old with her loving family, which is incredible when you realize that she weighed over a hundred pounds when mature and that large dogs typically don't live past twelve or thirteen years.

Working with her, I gained more breed knowledge, which reinforced to me the importance of researching breed characteristics before buying or training purebreds. She helped me refine my style of training. Inborn behaviors are hard—if not impossible—to modify, so I had to learn how to work around them.

Sierra lives on in the hearts and souls of her mom, Jenny, her dad Rick, and her brother Eric. Beyond the Rainbow Bridge, she growls, barks, and runs like the wind. If I close my eyes, I can see her loving, trusting face, and I thank God for the time I spent with her. She galloped into my heart, and she gallops still.

MICKEY DA MOOK

The call came from Gloria, who identified herself as the secretary to a vascular surgeon. Gloria asked if I would pick up, board, and train a dog for her boss. We made an appointment to start the process—I told her I would have to evaluate the dog's temperament and the issue at hand before I'd agree to board him.

Mickey da Mook—his owner was likely a Martin Scorsese fan—was a large one-year-old German shorthaired pointer with a deep muscular chest and narrow waist. I'm just over six feet tall: Most German shorthairs I'd worked with prior to him had only reached my mid-thigh at most, but Mickey's head was up to my belly button.

Having acquired Mickey from a rancher, the doctor held high hopes to hunt birds with the pointer. Instead he soon discovered that the dog was gun-shy, cringing at every shot fired. Mickey didn't like the sound of fireworks either.

So the doc wondered if training could help the dog get over its fear of gunfire. I told him that it was unlikely—it's one of the most difficult problems to undo. The best way to avoid it is to properly introduce hunting pups and young dogs to the sound of gunfire in the first place—at some distance and while the dog is distracted or occupied in an activity it enjoys.

Mickey's owner decided he would like me to work with the dog anyway. When I leashed and handled Mickey, he was powerful but good-natured, trying hard to please me. Agreeing to board and train him, I brought the magnificent, happy-go-lucky pointer home with me.

Midnight's eyes nearly popped out of their sockets when she saw his size. Still, she approached him with her characteristically hospitable smile and licked his chin. He smiled back. I crated him in our main living area where Aiko was sprawled. We let Mickey settle in.

Within an hour, the hunting dog was restless. He needed to be walked to release some of his vim and vigor. I put a nylon slip collar on him, leashed him, and loaded him into the SUV with Midnight and Aiko. Off we went to Papago Park, where we power walked four miles, covering ground as a pack.

Returning home, my pack leaders and I relaxed— Midnight and Aiko drank water and lay down on the cool tile. But Mickey just stood there, still trembling with surplus energy. This dog was wired.

I felt it best for his development to involve his owner in some of the training. The doc and I agreed to work with Mickey twice a week at neutral sites—places unfamiliar to the dog, i.e., not the dog's home or yard nor my home or yard. Mickey's territorial instincts would be suppressed in a neutral location. We chose a park close to the surgeon's home.

Back at our place, Mickey bonded with our pack. I walked him, worked him in obedience daily, and accelerated the sessions with the doctor. On our trips to Papago Park, I dearly wanted to let Mickey off-leash so he could fully discharge his pent-up power. But I knew that if he took off, Midnight and Aiko would not be able to keep up with him. I wasn't sure yet that Mickey would return on command after experiencing his newfound freedom. I had to bide my time.

There came a day he was ready to be tested. At the park, I dropped his leash, walked twenty feet away, and called him. I was nervous, but Mickey beelined to me and parked his butt in a perfect sit at my feet. There I stood with egg on my face. I picked up his leash, and we walked until no one was in sight. I dropped Mickey's six-foot lead and told him he was free. As I had suspected, with his powerful stride and intensity, Mickey left Midnight and Aiko in the dust. I muttered a prayer for his safety.

My dogs and I continued our trek while Mickey euphorically bounded in broad circles around us. I called him back after twenty minutes. He responded immediately and settled in front of me. I praised him, picked up his leash, and put water down. When he'd slaked his thirst, we headed back to the parking lot.

The next day, I unleashed him, and all went well. With patience, training, and lots of praise, even energetic dogs can be trusted to return when called if—and this is a big if—they have been well exercised, trained, and bonded with a pack. The exceptions to this rule are the serious prey-driven canines such as beagles, bloodhounds, and basset hounds, among others. Hounds in general have been bred to work independently of their owners and typically range further afield. They are off like a shot the instant they sight or smell prey.

As a handler with well-trained dogs, I take a dog off-leash if it's obedient and packed up, and if no one is in sight. But off-leash dogs are against many public regulations. Most, if not all, parks require dogs to be leashed at all times for the safety of the public, the dogs, and the wildlife.

If someone were to ask me to leash my dog, I would do it pronto. But the request rarely comes because as the top alpha of my pack, I'm alert and continually on the lookout for others. I call my dogs back, leash them, and put them in a sit-stay position before people approach.

Mickey da Mook was the most amazing German shorthair I ever met. I'll never forget his lopsided, goofy grin when he was introduced to Midnight and Aiko. Every day with Mickey, I wondered how the heck I'd expend his huge store of irrepressible energy. But by covering more and more ground, the way of the wolf pack worked its magic. Mickey never hunted with his owner, but he became an easier dog to have around when his owner learned the importance of keeping him well exercised through walks.

DOUBLE D'S
FEAR AGGRESSION

A middle-aged couple contacted me to help them with their dog Dakota, a Great Pyrenees. The large breed originated many centuries ago to protect sheep from predators in the Pyrenees Mountains between Spain and France. As I observed Dakota on my first visit, his owners told me their backstory. In search of a companion for their aging standard poodle, they had shopped at a pet store.

Staring at them with deep onyx eyes rimmed in lush black eyelashes was a Great Pyrenees puppy. The adorable white fluffball looked like a polar bear cub. Spending some time with him, the couple connected with the little Pyr and brought him home.

Their poodle, Seurat, had growled and barked at the intruder, but his vocalizations were for naught—the pup was undeterred. Dakota followed Seurat everywhere like a white shadow. The owners noticed that the pup didn't respond to his name being called, but since he trailed the poodle everywhere, the couple simply called Seurat when they wanted Dakota to come.

Testing by their veterinarian determined that Dakota was deaf. Informing the store where they had purchased him of the condition, the couple were told they could return him for store credit, but by then, the hook of love was embedded and the couple wouldn't part with him.

Seurat and Dakota eventually bonded. In the pack dynamic, the Great Pyr was docile, happy, and loving. Unfortunately, the old poodle got sick and was diagnosed with pervasive malignant cancer. The end followed quickly. With Seurat gone, the grown 140-pound Dakota lost his alpha leader who had also acted as his ears.

Dakota then startled at anything that entered his field of vision. He became increasingly bellicose and reactive to visual stimuli, including the approach of his owners. As his aggression escalated, his owners became fearful, and that was why they'd called me.

The contrast in Dakota's demeanor before and after Seurat's death was stark. It was clear that Dakota was distressed without Seurat, who had provided such great companionship. But it was more than just grief for the loss of his buddy that caused his alarming behavior. When awake, Dakota had watched Seurat like a hawk.

The Great Pyr had depended on Seurat's signals—via body posturing—to read the environment. If Seurat stood tall with a raised tail and chest out or moved his jaws as he barked, deaf Dakota—or DD as I sometimes called him—knew to be on guard. If Seurat was calm and comfortable, DD could relax.

Lacking the cues his companion had displayed, the insecure Dakota was constantly on alert. His routine was upset—he didn't know when it was time to do anything. This sent his anxiety through the roof, priming him to lash out. If he'd been a miniature breed, it might have been less frightening, but Dakota was *huge*.

I recommended that his owners should talk to their vet about prescribing something to lessen Dakota's anxiety. I then retrained the Great Pyr in basic obedience using broad hand and arm signals. Out of habit, I couldn't restrain my nonstop verbal praise, but realizing Dakota could not hear me, I redoubled my soothing physical strokes and ear scratches to reassure him.

Between medication dispensed by the veterinarian, mastering hand commands, and being rewarded with physical affection, DD calmed down and enjoyed our daily sessions. The owners watched what I did, got on board with the program, and practiced the exercises I assigned to them.

I suggested getting a puppy, preferably a female, for their pack. She could become Dakota's new ears. He could take his visual cues from her posture and activity just as he had with Seurat. DD's owners purchased a chocolate lab female they named Asha, which means "hope" in Sanskrit and "life" in Swahili. Asha shadowed

Dakota just like Dakota had once done to Seurat, and like Seurat, at first DD growled and barked in turn at Asha. In time, they grew attached to each other and subsequently got along well.

As DD's owners increased their use of hand signals to communicate with him, they slowly weaned him off the anti-anxiety medication he had been treated with. It took months of hard work. Beautiful Asha became DD's constant pal, and he followed her lead.

Every time the owners traveled and I boarded this canine odd couple, they moved as one through my house and pack. Dakota had a long and prosperous life, and when he passed away, his owners inquired whether they should get a new companion for Asha. I pointed out that Asha was an alpha female, and as a result, had no need of puppies or sidekicks because she was right where she wanted to be: queen of the household.

It had been a challenging case, but working together as a team, we were able to regain the chi and harmony in their household. Dakota taught me much about patience, posture, and the use of broad physical signals to replace or enhance vocal commands especially when dealing with anxious hearing-impaired animals.

Consistent physical affection to replace verbal praise can reassure a dog born into a seemingly silent world. I loved this special Great Pyr, and when my confidence wanes, I always recall Dakota's trust in my abilities. With a little hope, lots of love, and consistent work, anything is possible.

MAUS THE LITTLE
LOWRIDER

Another small dog that educated me in posturing was an alpha-male miniature dachshund named Mauser. I was hired to train "the Maus" when he was about ten weeks old by Dirk Cussler and his wife. Since the gentleman and his father, Clive, traveled frequently to research locations for the action-adventure novels they wrote together, the Maus often came to board at Bad Dogs.

As always, Midnight and Aiko greeted the hearty ten-pound black-and-brown dog when he arrived. Maus readily followed them out the dog door to the yard to do his business. Housebreaking can sometimes be an issue for a young alpha in a group. Wanting to establish themselves in the hierarchy, they may mark their scent by peeing in the house. Other little alphas may in turn pee in the same spot. But little Maus fell in line with my pack leaders and emulated their good behavior.

Though small in stature and weight, Maus possessed a big personality with an overabundance of dachshund determination. He was a quick study, and despite his short legs and lowrider body, he loved our walks in the desert no matter how far we went.

I always kept him on leash because as a hound breed, he had a fierce prey drive. The little wiener dog never complained, balked, or wanted to be picked up. He always stepped boldly with a smile on his face instead, his tail sticking straight up while his legs pumped at two to three times the speed of the larger breeds.

Given that he was allowed on the furniture at Dirk's house, Maus was permitted to sit next to me on the couch while I relaxed after a hike. When he first started boarding with me, I would pick him up and place him on the sofa, then gently put him back on the floor afterward so he wouldn't jump off the couch and damage his elongated torso. But between eight-to-twelve-months of age, little Maus's muscles had become so well developed from the hiking that he was able to leap up on the sofa and down to the floor without any discomfort or strain.

At the end of the evening, I would put him on our bed where he'd burrow under the covers, roll onto his back, and stick his front legs straight up to hold the covers off him while he slept soundly. Dachshund translates from German as "badger dog." These long, low dogs were bred to hunt badgers holed up in underground dens. You have to be one tough cookie to confront a cornered badger, which explained why Maus was calm and comfortable when tucked under the bedcovers—being in tight quarters with other animals in the dark was innate for a dachshund. And it was a plus that he would warm up the bed for my frosty feet during Arizona's chilly winter nights.

It was fascinating to observe the small dog's power to intimidate and confound a much larger dog. Sitting next to me, Maus would posture assertively at other dogs who wandered over and approached the couch looking for attention. I had to condition him out of that pushy behavior because he was terrorizing Dakota, the deaf beta male Great Pyr. We worked through this issue consistently with me employing lots of praise when Maus dropped his severe stance above Dakota's cowering bulk.

Back at Maus's home, coyotes roamed the washes at night throughout the estates, leaping with ease to the top of six-foot border walls around the properties—a great vantage point from which to scout for (and hunt) rabbits. Dirk had built an outdoor enclosure for Maus to access through a dog door from the master bedroom. The run was protected all around by chicken wire so that the prowling coyotes wouldn't have the opportunity to mistake Maus for dinner.

My usual practice for coyote deterrence was to spray wolf or bear urine on clients' walls every six feet, but during the rainy season it would get washed away. The Maus was lucky to have owners who built a secure enclosure for his safety when he relieved himself during the night.

Maus has since passed, but memories of his big-dog-spirit-in-a-little-body exploits still have him walking with my pack in my dreams. I chuckle recalling his lowrider gait—those short legs pumping away like pistons in a race car at full throttle to keep up with the bigger dogs. He was a special little guy. And every time I visit a bookstore or the library and see a new book by his owner, I get to enjoy the continuing sagas of tireless human adventurers that so many of us read and revere.

STRYDER THE LAB-RABBIT

A woman living in the McCormick Ranch area of Scottsdale hired me to train her young Labrador retriever. As I arrived for my first visit at her home, she pulled in at the same time in a swanky new Mercedes-Benz.

Exiting the token of success wearing tight designer workout attire, she greeted me with a disarming smile. When I asked where the dog was, the woman who looked like a supermodel led me through her picture-perfect house past her two immaculate children and out a back door. She explained that she kept the dog outside because her son had asthma.

A fenced-in pool area took up half of the backyard. The other half was a grassy domain for free-roaming bunnies and the yellow Lab named Stryder. He hopped up and pummeled me with affection. His eyes were brown with golden edges. I collared and leashed him for evaluation. After an hour of getting to know him, I was full of sympathy and compassion for the sweet, lonely dog. Stryder needed to be packed up, and not with the ever-increasing number of rabbits he had been cohabitating with.

At my next session with the client, I broached the subject of incorporating Stryder into her family pack. I asked about the severity of her son's asthma and if there were some spaces in the house where Stryder might interact with family but where her son could readily avoid. She resisted the subject, ending the discussion quickly. It was nonnegotiable: The dog had to remain outdoors.

I tried my best to enlighten her that because dogs are pack animals, a dog kept outside alone will forever be insecure and unhappy, and all the training in the world wouldn't fix that. To be clear, I reiterated: Without the structure and companionship of his pack, Stryder would always present behavior problems.

My client remained unmoved. I countered with a new proposal: Could I take the dog off her hands? At first, she turned me down, but after I had several more sessions with Stryder, she relinquished him to me. Our first stop on the way home was the vet's office. Stryder hadn't had any inoculations yet, so we got that started, and I scheduled a date for him to be neutered.

Several hundred dollars later, I brought him home to meet Midnight and Aiko. I told my poochies to give a warm welcome to Stryder, a seventy-eight-pound "wascally wabbit" in a yellow Lab costume. Damn if I didn't learn a lot with that tribe!

Stryder never licked people but would sniff them up close and wiggle his whiskers. Instead of striding like his name would suggest, he often hopped. He was burly yet gentle and didn't know his own strength. He needed us to lead him into the canine world. Stryder never showed anger toward other canines, but few dogs could dominate him either. He respected Midnight and Aiko and mirrored their behaviors.

Every day I would get up before dawn and take this dog pack—plus whatever dogs were boarding with us—to Papago Park for a power walk. In the rosy-orange glow of sunrise, we'd hike and chase Stryder's jackrabbit "cousins" for an hour, kickstarting our metabolisms and generating endorphins that gave us a great start each day.

I worked long and hard with Stryder that year. The first time I let him off-leash was not until months later when we were in Crested Butte, Colorado, where we went to escape the brutal summer heat of Phoenix. There we would recharge our city-life batteries in the relative wilderness.

On a ski-resort mountain at an elevation of 9,500 feet, we all walked up a dirt road, huffing and puffing from the altitude. I unclipped Stryder and told him he was free. He was off like a shot. For a brief moment, Aiko tried to corral him, but Stryder blew past Aiko like he was standing still. Midnight barked a warning but didn't pursue.

Stryder ran like a cheetah on the African savanna. It wasn't long before he was out of sight ahead of us. After a minute of wondering if we would ever see him again, we heard twigs snapping and saw the underbrush swaying in the overgrown area that flanked the ski slope. Stryder had doubled back through the brush and burst out hurtling toward us.

Stryder

The moment was captured on camera. The photo of him leaping out of the woods, grinning from ear-to-ear with his tongue rolling out of his mouth, became that year's Christmas card with the inscription "Joy" written below.

Stryder was the first and only Lab-bunny I ever worked with, and I thank the universe for having had him in my life. It really doesn't matter where you come from or who raised you: With love, patience, persistence, and the right pack, you can find joy.

FERN IN A BOX

A couple with an older puppy that the wife inherited from her parents called me for help. Long story short, the woman's parents had kept the pup in a tiny crate—more like a box or a shoe box—from day one in the garage by itself for two months before shuffling it to their daughter.

When I got to their condominium and met the mouthy, blaming, cynical husband and his timid, passive-aggressive wife, I should have distracted them both, stolen the young dog away, trained it, and placed it in a good home.

Instead, the professional and eternal optimist in me took charge and within twenty minutes had the miniature poodle-Lhasa apso mix—all nine pounds of her—performing sit, stay, come, and heel like a seasoned circus performer. The petite cutie was named Fern.

I hoped the couple was paying attention and would follow my lead by practicing some positivity with the routines I showed them, but during the second session, their chronic kvetching and negativity wore on me.

For Fern, I added down and down-stay to the obedience mix, and once again she mastered the new commands while the couple floundered as though they were stupefied or were robots whose electronics had been short-circuited. They did everything bass-ackward to what I was doing, and when mildly redirected, they quit and sulked.

Driving away after sessions like that, I used to agonize over what I could have done differently with my show-and-tell shtick, but now I get angry and begrudge those folks the air we share. Worst of all, the couple still kept Fern separated from the family in the same Lilliputian box, either downstairs in the kitchen or outside on the patio next to their feces-covered yard. They offered lame excuses for not picking up and disposing of the poor dog's poop.

I gave them a list of instructions: stop free-feeding Fern and feed her just two times a day, walk and train her daily in their gated enclave, and get Fern a larger crate. Looking at me like I was insane, they sputtered and gave me grief about why that would be impossible. I bit my tongue and scheduled another session. They called later in the week to cancel, and the jerk of a man told me they were going to sell Fern on Craigslist.

Puppies and dogs need socializing, not compart-mentalization. They'll only learn to be well-adjusted and secure when they're with their pack. When isolated, their growth, development, and maturation are arrested, not to mention it's an incredibly sad life.

The dog those indolent people needed was a stuffed animal from Toys "R" Us, and quite frankly, they probably would have set a plushie on fire with their cigarettes. All I could do about the situation was pray, which is what I do every day for most dogs that end up with half-assed people who couldn't grow weeds in a pot filled with fertilizer.

TALKING S#!T

By now you're aware that I take many walks with dogs. On those jaunts I carry poop bags and pay attention to my surroundings. Long ago I stopped counting how many times I saw a dog take a dump somewhere in public, and the owner at the other end of their leash continued on their way like they were the King or Queen of England and it was beneath them to pick up after their pooch.

My mom walked daily. As she aged and the area's population grew around her, the accumulation of street garbage annoyed her to no end. She would rant and rail about it. I'm of like mind that trash is an irritating sight and smell, not to mention detrimental to public health.

In these stressful times of uncertainty and discord, I believe that if we all did our part to clean up our little corners of the world, we would make things a little better for ourselves and our neighbors. So I swore to myself that on my walks I would aim to pick up three things in addition to my dog's waste—and I'd try not to complain about it.

Unfortunately, there is all manner of rubbish lying around. The more I pick up, the more I spot. In the past I would sometimes come across used hypodermic needles and pick them up (carefully) so children wouldn't find them and hurt themselves. When I got home, I would take all the garbage I'd accrued and dispose of it properly in the alley trash bins. Then I'd sit in the backyard sipping coffee while also enjoying that warm feeling that comes from making my surroundings a little cleaner.

So do yourself and the world a favor—tend to your dog's waste in your own yard (this keeps the fly population down), and on your daily walk with Fido, please pick up after them. Make time to stroll your neighborhood with your furry friend and meet and greet your neighbors with a friendly smile (and a wee bag of litter newly acquired).

Take pride that you've made your community brighter. And if you pass me on the street and my mouth is moving, rest assured, I'm not grousing about garbage or dog poop. Talking s#!t is a waste of time, and I have to let it go.

ROMEO AND THE GIFT THAT KEEPS ON GIVING

The phone rang. A plea was made. A time was scheduled. I knocked on the door at the specified hour. Those were the sounds and steps of animal rescue, a cause near and dear to me and my partner Lana.

A sturdy soul with thick lenses answered the door. I thought of her as Mrs. Magoo—not the disk jockey but rather a female version of Mr. Magoo, an old cartoon character who was blind as a bat—and from then on, she was Mrs. Magoo to me. A few pleasantries were exchanged, and Mrs. Magoo invited us into her home.

A wall of cat stench assaulted us as we wove our way past stacks of newspapers, magazines, and boxes. It became obvious that her primary calling was cat

145

rescue—bless her heart—followed by a secondary compulsion for hoarding. She'd been a saint to take in homeless creatures.

Behind a closed slider door, guttural growls emanated from the kitchen. Mrs. Magoo informed us that the source of the snarling was born under an abandoned building, and his mother unfortunately had been euthanized.

Cracking the door open, I saw a chocolate-brown puppy pressed into the corner of the room, quaking in fear at our presence. Instead of immediately barging in, I closed the door and conferred with Lana on our plan. Mrs. Magoo overheard and agreed that the plan was sound. She had superlative resolve and assured us we would succeed—or was it simply that she wouldn't permit us to accept defeat?

I reopened the door, and we slipped in with coos of praise. Lana and I approached from opposite sides and sat next to the terrified eleven-week-old Lab-pit bull puppy. We wormed our butts up against his while continuing to chatter in sweet, high-pitched tones that signified affection. Eventually, his trembling subsided, and we stole glances at his big brown, gold-tinged eyes that sucked us in like black holes in space.

Within minutes, he owned us while continuing to growl at decibels unparalleled for an eighteen-pound puppy. My eyes met Lana's, and we nodded in silent agreement to do whatever was necessary to save the little guy. I knew he would likely fail any shelter's aggression test, so we consulted once again with Mrs. Magoo who unequivocally wanted us to get the nuisance pup out of her cat rescue and skedaddle.

Clearly we had her approval. I picked him up as securely as I could, and we made our way out of the kitchen, back through the winding trails among clutter, and out of the house. I put him in a crate in the back of my car then turned to Lana. Her birthday was near, and I sang "Happy Birthday to You."

She named her birthday present Romeo. Once we got the little bugger home, we strategized on how to reduce his defensive growling. Lana believes in the power of love. She figured that if her love was able to lessen *my* growling persona, then the puppy's snarls would be a piece of cake. And like Mrs. Magoo, Lana doesn't give up.

Our pack came to investigate the new addition, sniffed Romeo in his crate, then went back to their routine. With our goal to keep the mood calm and unstimulating, we walked away to give him space. We wanted him to get used to being in a new home and to be curious about his new pack. I gave him regular breaks from the crate.

At three o'clock in the morning, Romeo threw up in his crate. I got up and dealt with it. He continued to growl at us off-and-on for three weeks but eventually stopped. He became a fine addition to our pack, and when fully grown tipped the scales at eighty-two pounds. Though Romeo stopped his knee-jerk reaction of growling at all humans, he didn't hesitate to snarl at anyone he perceived as threatening Lana. For strangers who approached too closely to our property, Romeo demonstrated his deep, deafening bark.

When we took him to a Huntington Beach dog park in Southern California on one of our getaways, he loved romping off-leash and sniffing the abundant scents.

Spooked at first by the thunderous sound of crashing surf, he grew more accustomed to it as he cruised up and down the beach distracted by all the dogs. Despite all the activity, Romeo excelled at responding to our commands better than the purebreds he was running with.

Another time on an October day, rain stormed into Phoenix propelled by near-hurricane gales racing north from Baja California. After the front blew past, the ground was saturated with moisture, and the air temperature had dropped significantly.

Since we had the day off, Lana and I took advantage of the rare weather by taking Romeo to Papago Park for a mid-afternoon hike. We entered the park south of the National Guard compound which keeps enveloping land off the 52nd Street entrance like red-hot lava overtaking estates on the big island of Hawaii.

Striding in on the access road, we let Romeo off his leash to check pee-mail and stalk some "wascally wabbits." It wasn't as bad as it sounds—the "wabbits" were jackrabbits that run like the wind and no animals can catch them. I kept hoping that Romeo would have an epiphany about that and stop chasing them, but his prey drive was too strong.

The sky was robin's-egg blue, the flora were glistening from the rain, and the scent of every living thing was overwhelming. Romeo's nose led him over the rough terrain.

Lana and I laughed, held hands, and strolled together watching him revel in the impromptu adventure. Within a half mile, we decided to leash him since we feared for his well-being. Over an hour's walk later, we arrived back at the car and drove home. Not having done that long a hike since May, we all succumbed to a catnap.

Sometime after rousing from my nap, I noticed Romeo licking his right rear paw. Examining the irritated section of his leg, I found a gash about three inches long and one inch wide which was alarming. It was the weekend, and our vet's office was closed until Monday, so we dropped him off at the emergency vet clinic on Hayden Road to get his injury taken care of.

They anesthetized him, cleaned his wound, stitched him up, and called us when he was ready to go home. When we got there, the anesthesia hadn't fully worn off yet, so I squatted around his eighty-two-pound frame, scooped him up, carried him to the car and lifted him into the backseat to the soundtrack of my creaking knees and back. My aging skeleton endured, and I silently thanked my rigorous workout regime.

At home we extricated him from the car and left him in his bed on the floor of our bedroom where he could sleep off the drugs comfortably. Lana and I each slept with one eye open that night, but Romeo made it through easily, ate his breakfast, agreeably ingested his medications, and even managed a short stroll around the block to relieve himself.

He peed here, there, and everywhere, but unfortunately he couldn't produce any number two. Between the anesthesia and the pain meds he had been given, he was bound up tighter than new bongo drum skins.

For five days, he was required to be on tramadol (a painkiller), acepromazine (a sedative) and cephalexin (an antibiotic). Once these prescriptions ran out, we had to place the dreaded "cone from hell" around his neck to quash his urge to lick the itchy, healing wound.

I still took him for daily walks and we kept him as calm as possible for two weeks. Then the next week, Romeo had had enough of his neckwear. He scraped the cone against every door, wall, table, chair, and object he thought could rid him of that infernal contraption. He managed to get to the wound from time to time, so we didn't have to worry about taking the stitches out because he'd already performed that task. Who knew he was medically inclined?

The healing process of a beloved pet can be a challenge, but when our Romeo was completely healed, the sun shone a little brighter and our smiles came easier. The bottom line is we loved him dearly. A rescue dog is the gift that keeps on giving.

If you're thinking about adding a dog to your household, consider going to a shelter or through a rescue organization to find the right companion animal for you. Keep in mind they are in a rescue facility because they've had a rough start. They're waiting for the other shoe to drop or for being abandoned or abused again, so give them time to trust you.

If you already have several dogs at home, you might want to introduce a new rescue to them at a neutral site like a local park before bringing them home. The introductions at a neutral place tend to go smoother because it reduces territorial defensiveness. Then going back to the established pack's turf is easier.

The best way to progress with rescues is to assess their strengths and tailor your interactions with them accordingly. Once you demonstrate you're in it for the long haul with love, patience, and security, they'll come around. It can be hard work, but in the end, much that's worth a damn is hard work.

A NOTE ON LITTLE DOGS

Awakened to a downpour, I heard the rain pitter-patter on our patio's tin roof like frenzied cats tap dancing after downing triple-shot espressos. As we drank our coffee and perused the local morning newspaper, the Arizona monsoon skittered away leaving a gunmetal gray sky that kept the harsh summer sun at bay. It was a glorious morning—as good as it gets in Arizona in late summer.

Wanting to take full advantage of the conditions, I dressed in bike shorts, tank top, and cross trainers for a short power walk with Romeo. No one else was around, so I started with him off-leash. He scurried from scent to scent. The air was fresh and laden with moisture.

Having worked with tracking dogs from time to time, I've observed that after a rainstorm—if it isn't torrential—scents get freshened and magnified. Romeo was in hog heaven, nose-to-the-ground sniffing while trundling to a new spot, marking turf, and sniffing some more.

Because those in the neighborhood were waking up and venturing outdoors, I leashed him as we covered more ground. The temperature was in the low 70s—rare for the time of year—so I kept him motoring forward and keeping up with me. All the birds who had disappeared prior to the storm were back, fluffing and preening their feathers while chirping to beat the band. A tall young runner jogged past, earbuds jutting from her ears, and she flashed a brief smile while lip-syncing to Beyoncé. A swarthy jock type sprinted in the middle of the street, barefoot.

I encountered others out walking and being tugged hither and yon by their dogs darting from smell to smell. A young woman was pulled by two small dogs at the end of their extendable leashes. Her pooches yapped away as if they were Paul Revere warning that the British were coming.

Another woman was being dragged at leash's end by a dachshund-basset hound cross whose tail was erect and curved like a furry scimitar. I made a mental note about how important it is to train obedience in small dogs when they're young, because most are born alphas, and if coddled (as small dogs often are) and put in the lead position frequently, their alpha tendencies are amplified. Consequently, they become problem barkers or worse when they mature, like little tyrants.

When I showed up at homes where two or more little dogs lived, the cacophony of shrill barking was almost insurmountable when trying to converse with the client. At such times, I would lie down on the floor in the foyer or living room. The little yappers would immediately stop their uproar because in dog communication I was showing complete submission and therefore no longer the threat they felt they needed to alert their household to.

Some little dogs are descended from circus dogs and often get bored if not trained and encouraged to perform. Training is essential for all dogs, regardless of size, or else when they mature, their poor behaviors during puppyhood become entrenched and more challenging to eliminate.

I once trained a miniature poodle for an older gentleman and his family who owned and ran a large auto dealership. The guy was used to barking orders and watching people jump. Though his wife and family worked well with me, he did not. He would whack the dog across the muzzle with his finger or hand, and when he refused to follow my guidance, I told him if he couldn't stop hitting his dog, I would discontinue the training. He wouldn't budge, so we had no more sessions.

I can't watch animals being abused, and the vision of the man's hands and wrists covered in fresh bites and scabs of old wounds still haunts me. You should *never* hit a dog with your hand or fist, under any condition, unless your intent is to create a biter. Corrections should instead be administered by tugs on collars hooked up to leashes and should preferably be learned under the supervision of a professional dog trainer showing you how to perform the correction properly.

Human hands should only be used to administer affection, love, and praise. Proper training establishes good communication and social hierarchy. Training teaches dogs to listen and obey you in any crisis. To own and live with an untrained dog is to squander an opportunity to become a better person and to develop a greater bond with the dog.

ROMEO AND JULIET

As our aging Romeo bravely battled Cushing's disease (a condition caused by overactive adrenal glands and indicated by increased appetite, water consumption, and urination), we resolved to get a puppy companion for him. I hoped the addition of a new little one might infuse a revitalizing spirit in Romeo and extend his life.

Spotting an ad in the *Arizona Republic* for Lab–shepherd mix pups, I called and arranged to inspect the litter. Planning to pick a smaller female with a beta disposition, I drove west across the Salt River Valley—the basin in which Phoenix sits—toward farm country, with the love of my life Lana by my side. Shortly we were viewing three females and eight males that were seven-and-a-half weeks old.

Testing the temperaments of the females, I determined all were alphas. I was ready to pass and head home, but Lana liked a little one with white back paws and a white splotch on her chest. When on her back during the testing, the pup had remained still for about fifteen seconds before squirming, indicating a mild-to-medium alpha. Captivated with her diminutive size and beautiful markings, Lana fell in love right on the spot. This happens. I had no problem with it—love wins.

We handed the lady cash and headed home with Lana cradling the pup like a baby and cooing and sweet-talking her. Since the little fluffball was to be Romeo's companion, Lana named her Juliet. Upon arriving home, we immediately crated Juliet so she and Romeo could smell each other without physical contact and so she could get used to her new environment and her new pack.

Puppies need to spend as much time as possible with their pack so they can learn the group's activity and schedule. Instinctively they'll attempt to mirror pack behavior. Years before when Lana and I had acquired Romeo at eleven-weeks old, I trained him to go into his crate with the command Kennel Up.

With Juliet, after an hour, we let her out of her crate to roam in the fenced backyard. She leapt, tripped, rolled, and frolicked with unfettered joy. When she approached Romeo, he growled and walked away with disdain—a normal initial response for an old dog in this situation.

The first night, I crated Juliet next to my side of the bed so she could see, smell, and hear us. Romeo went to sleep on the floor. Juliet's crate was small, just twice her puppy size, and it was close enough to me that I would be able to hear her when she whimpered to go out.

As we slept, Juliet yipped when she couldn't hold it any longer. I heard her and took her outside to relieve herself, which she did promptly. She was about two months old, yet she had lasted four hours before needing to go out. I would have expected about three hours, so she did great. When she peed outside, I praised her. I carried her back inside, stroking and soothing her on the way back to the crate.

We took Juliet to the veterinarian for shots. Usually, they give a series of combined shots over the course of six-to-eight weeks to protect puppies against the serious diseases of distemper, hepatitis, parvovirus, para-influenza (kennel cough), and rabies. We didn't take Juliet off our property or let her interact with any other dogs except Romeo until all necessary shots had been administered. By then she was sixteen-weeks old.

After that, Juliet and I ventured out to walk. An alpha female, she initially resisted walking at a heel—she balked like a mercurial major league pitcher in the seventh inning. Alphas like to lead, not heel. I bit my tongue. She wasn't ready yet, so instead I played ball with her in the backyard. She picked up on fetch and liked it. We did that for a few weeks and then practiced obedience—sit, stay, come—again.

She began to acquiesce to my commands, and I praised her with "good girl, good girl, good girl." I tried walking with her again. We covered one block for a few days, then two blocks, and over time increased the distance to two miles while she heeled at a brisk pace.

Eventually, I was able to walk her and Romeo together until the Cushing's disease got the upper hand with him. Then I walked them separately—first Romeo, whose walks declined in length and pace, then Juliet, who would walk further and faster. With her irrepressible enthusiasm for hikes, Juliet became my live-in personal trainer who gets me up and going.

While her baby teeth were giving her pain, Juliet tried to chew various cables going in and out of our house, so I wrapped them in aluminum foil. That stopped her. We held nylon bones for her to chew while she lay next to us on the couch, winding down with some TV at the end of the day. Finally, all her baby teeth fell out, replaced by the adult versions that would settle in and form part of her imposing German shepherd jawline. She dug holes in the backyard that I filled with her feces and covered in dirt because dogs won't dig where their waste is located.

Beautiful little green-eyed Juliet kept evolving. She tried flirting with the elder Romeo by prancing coquettishly up to him, but he grumbled, indifferent to her charms. She continued to sleep through the night next to me in her crate on the floor. When we let Romeo into the backyard to relieve himself, she followed and mirrored his behavior. We crated her anytime we left the house.

When Juliet was four months old, Romeo stopped growling at her and even initiated some slow play. Training Juliet to follow commands at a distance, I worked her successfully up to six feet quickly, then gradually pushed her out to following commands at twenty feet away from me. That was her limit at five-and-a-half months old. If I tried commanding her beyond that distance, she didn't respond. I had to be patient with her, respecting her limits. She wanted me within twenty feet of her because that was when she felt the security of her pack.

At six months old, she was incredibly obedient on- and off-leash. As she matured physically, she gained more confidence. When the locale permitted it, I would command You're Free To The Left (or Right), and she would wander ahead or to the side, enjoying our power walk.

Eyes peeled on the horizon, I called her back if someone or something was up ahead. She came back to me like Lassie, running as fast as the wind. I would leash her and call her a good girl over and over while her eyes glistened with devotion. She was our darling.

Then Romeo took a turn for the worse. To avoid unnecessarily prolonging his life given his good days were dwindling, I took him off his meds for Cushing's disease. For pain, I gave him hemp cannabidiol (CBD, the non-psychoactive component in cannabis) in dog biscuits and from the liquid drops that I used myself for arthritis.

We indulged him with the treats he loved to chew — raw beef bones — that ordinarily weren't part of his diet. Lana and I agreed not to let him suffer. When he had difficulty getting up and moving about, we took him to the vet one last time to be euthanized. We were crushed.

When I got home and released Juliet from her crate, she searched frantically for Romeo. The joy and exuberance in her faded. She began growling at people, friends, and family who came to the house. She was mourning the loss of her buddy and mentor just as much as we were. I ramped up her walks and played ball more often with her in the backyard, but her puppy playfulness was gone.

A FEAR-BOUND
AUSTRALIAN SHEPHERD

Meanwhile, I trained dogs across town in Sun City. I had an appointment with a lady whose Australian shepherd rescue was afraid of everything. The older woman had recently recovered from a severe illness and was regaining her equilibrium while also endeavoring to love this terrified dog, a beautiful brown and black Aussie weighing approximately forty-five pounds.

She said he was a stray who had been abandoned in the desert near Tucson and was thought to be about two years old. She called him Snuggles.

I gave her a collar and lead and lay down on her living room floor while she leashed him, brought him over to me, and then handed me the lead. He tucked his tail as I rose to my feet and began performing my basic obedience routine—issuing the monotonal commands sit, stay, and come all while praising him in a singsong, high-pitched voice. He performed admirably but exhibited no joy or positive response to the physical and verbal praise.

After forty-five minutes, I had his owner work with him. She did several turns around the living room, her energy fading, so I relieved her of the leash. I told her that the Aussie was a beta male in need of daily walks and consistent work if he was to evolve past his earlier fearful and abusive life.

The woman hesitated to commit to any course of training sessions but promised to walk Snuggles daily and practice obedience. She agreed to one more single session in a month or two to get feedback on her and Snuggles' progress. I let the dog off the leash, and he bolted into her bedroom to hide in his corner.

About six weeks later, I arrived with my dog Juliet in tow, put the car windows down, and commanded her to stay in the car. My client let me in the house where I leashed Snuggles and brought him outside to my car, opened the door, and called Juliet—already leashed—to come. I walked around the block with both dogs heeling—Snuggles on my left and Juliet on my right. Any time I stopped, both assumed a sit position. I lavished praise on them both.

Returning from the walk, I took both dogs to the lady's backyard where I let Juliet off-leash and commanded her to go play. I dropped Snuggles' lead for him to drag around. I threw a ball for Juliet to fetch, and Snuggles ran after her as she chased it.

After the third round of this, Juliet brought the ball to him as he anxiously eyed—from a distance of twenty feet—both humans watching him: the frail caring woman and the loud alpha male (me) who reminded him of whoever had instilled his terrors.

I prompted Juliet to keep playing with him, so she cavorted around the rocky yard occasionally sniffing and laying scent. Snuggles began to exhibit a little cheer. When the one-and-a-half-hour session was up, I put water down for the dogs and called it quits. Juliet and I rode off into the guts of the city heading to our abode where we knew love.

The vision of Snuggles' spooked eyes burned in my mind, but I believed if we could get him to a point where he didn't flinch at every sound and movement, Juliet and I could reteach him.

Not long after that second visit, the client called to tell me that, sadly, her illness had returned. She asked if I would take Snuggles as my own since she could no longer walk him and because she had seen how much he came alive when Juliet was there. Lana and I adopted the Aussie, renaming him RJ—short for Romeo Jr.

I walked him and Juliet daily at a heel for one-and-a-half to two miles on city streets, allowing each to stop, sniff, and water the roses occasionally. The stops were necessary for RJ to mark turf. If he ever got separated from us, he would be able to sniff his way back to his new pack's home base.

Juliet continued on her emotional journey. Her mourning period for Romeo was extensive, but RJ's addition to the pack put her back on track. Thankfully, she took to the role of mentor for RJ, teaching him to enjoy play and spontaneity.

Romeo Jr. (RJ)

When I trained RJ, he performed everything out of fear with his tail tucked under his belly like it was glued there, but he responded gradually through much practice, consistency, and praise (verbal and physical).

Given his history of abuse, I had to tone down my command and correction voice with him and supersize my praise for everything he did correctly. Lana worked to alleviate his bad memories created by the past abuse, giving him nightly hugs, kisses, and coat brushings to reassociate human touch with pleasure.

Eventually he began to relax and blossom. His tail wasn't tucked all the time, indicating a decrease of his constant anxiety. Now when approached, he doesn't slink away in terror but rather responds with affection. His confidence has risen along with his tail, which he now carries fluffed out like a proud peacock. He prances and wags his tail when Lana and I arrive home. It's a sight to behold.

On a two-week vacation to Seaside, Oregon, I went to the beach daily, let well-trained Juliet off-leash, and dropped RJ's leash. I told them, "You're free, walk the beach." They frolicked, chased gulls, darted in and out of the Pacific Ocean, and came like the wind when called.

Juliet performed perfectly, but occasionally RJ balked. His layers of fear that hadn't yet been shed thwarted a consistent response to commands. So I would tell him to stay, praise him, and slowly walk toward him while gathering up his leash little by little.

One time as they dashed in and out of the water, an oncoming rush of the sea pushed a big wave up on the beach and swept off RJ's collar and leash. Though it took us by surprise, I knew I had to stay calm for RJ. Praising him in happy tones, I then called him to come and turned around and walked back toward our rental house. I could see he was following Lana, Juliet, and me.

As we got in view of the cottage several blocks away, he raced off. When we arrived shortly after, there he was waiting for us on the porch.

All dogs, alphas and betas alike, are searching for demonstrative alphas to lead them in positive directions. Fearful dogs and abused rescues are especially relieved when they're treated calmly and when they sense that their alpha leader protects them and their pack.

Progress does not occur on a straight line forward—there will be relapses. And as much as you might naturally tend to freak out or lose your temper, try to resist this. It doesn't help.

Though RJ still has some pockets of fear, for the most part he loves praise so much that he works for it happily. He no longer requires daily training after we return from our morning pack walks. His only persistent issue is digging, not only holes in the backyard but—believe it or not—quarter-sized holes in our polished concrete floors!

He has scraped out a divot at the entrance to the bathroom (where we've now gated the doorway) and another between our kitchen and living room. Lana cleaned them up, and we patched and repainted them both. We put a throw rug over the repaired hole in the kitchen-living room entryway, and thus far, we're good. Yet we must be prepared every year when we reseed the lawn with rye for winter, because that triggers RJ's digging, and he's right back at it again if we let him outside.

When you work with rescues, it's a guessing game as to what specifically has happened to them before you met them. My observations of other rescues and RJ's behavior point to him being left inside somewhere, possibly penned, for far too long periods of time.

If you have a rescue that has been abused or abandoned in the past, exercise them, walk them, and expose them to various new situations in little steps. When they reveal their fears, put some distance between them and the stimulus, and work with them on the basic tasks in a place where they're comfortable.

Juliet, Lana, and RJ

Give them praise and treats when they've done the behaviors you want to become habit. As they perform these tasks, bring them closer and closer to what caused them grief, keeping up the rewards when they've responded well to your commands. If you do this repeatedly with patience and praise, you'll see progress.

On a recent visit to Papago Park, I let Juliet off-leash and dropped RJ's lead so he could have some freedom. We hiked for about two miles among red rock formations in the scenic desert. Though RJ played with Juliet and gamboled about, he was noticeably more restrained than on his home turf.

He kept close watch on Lana and me, probably because he had been abandoned in a desert and was afraid to be left behind again. This is a negative association our sweet Aussie may never let go. Do you blame him?

PIERCE H RUSSELL JR

ROCCO THE RUNAWAY

One morning after Juliet, RJ, and I completed our powerful pack walk, we headed back into the house to see Lana off to work. Right then, our neighbor, a blond in her late thirties, hightailed it into our driveway chasing Rocco, her felonious escapee of a miniature pinscher-Chihuahua mix. The diminutive dog barked up a storm while fashionably attired Michelle tottered on four-inch-high heels imploring her new, unruly rescue to come.

Leaving our dogs in the house, Lana and I entered the fray. I didn't try to catch or even reach for Rocco. I didn't plead or yell at him. Those actions don't get a dog to come. Instead, Lana squatted while I lay down to show submission to the scared, demonstrative alpha. He circled me warily, and we spoke to him in praise tones.

I suggested to Michelle that we should use the power of the pack to lure Rocco home rather than chase him. I got up and asked Lana and Michelle to follow me and stay close behind, then I led the way slowly across the street. When I got to Michelle's house, I opened the door for the ladies, and I'll be damned if the nervous little male—yapping all the while—didn't follow them into the house.

Once they were in, I closed the door. Lana and Michelle soon reemerged so they could head to work, Michelle effusive with thanks. Our quiet morning had taken an unexpected turn, but when life throws curveballs, it helps to roll with them if you can, rather than kicking and screaming.

Sticking with their pack is essential to canines, and that's why I didn't try to catch Rocco and sternly correct him. I just gathered the little group of us and covered ground to his home. He followed our makeshift pack because it's an allure to a solitary dog—a magnetic pull that tapped into his need to survive. By packing up with us, he returned to safety and security.

DISPATCHED ANGELS

I n the early 1990s, I exercised dogs at Los Olivos Park in north-central Phoenix. There, all the dog owners and their pets hung out together with the dogs off-leash. It was fascinating to watch puppies try to emulate adult dogs while romping and playing as the sun peeked over the horizon, stretched out its rays, and ascended.

An older couple, John and Ina, walked their German shorthaired pointer with us. I recall their delight in viewing the brilliant sunrise. We lost contact after I started hiking regularly at Papago Park. Years later on an outing with Romeo to Los Olivos Park, I reencountered John and asked him how he and his wife were doing. In his eighties, he responded, "We're waiting to die."

Once in great shape, Ina was bedridden and tended to daily by a nurse. John expressed sorrow over the passing of their last dog Misty. I commiserated with him and asked—given they obviously loved dogs—why didn't they get a rescue dog to love and invigorate them in the last stage of their life?

I walked there again a few months later. John stopped me and enthusiastically told me they had acquired a small female rescue that was joined at the hip with Ina. Since then, Ina had been inspired to walk around their pool every day, pushing her walker with the dog by her side. John beamed like the sunrise of yesteryear as he regaled me with the story.

I firmly believe that dogs are put here on earth to love us blindly whether we have good days or bad. To me, they're angels dispatched from a higher power to show us how to love no matter what. Some of us are so damaged during childhood that we need these spiritual mentors to show us how to get on with living positively. If we spurn their attentions and fail to reciprocate, we may unwittingly perpetuate the sad conditions we endure.

As my dad lay dying in a hospital bed, he fought with every ounce of his remaining energy to criticize me. I told him I loved him and forgave him. Concerning my mother—with whom I got along much more easily—I had more time to say goodbye. I loved her the best I could and forgave her for all the "I love you, buts" that had preceded our dialogues. Forgiving my parents before they passed away was cathartic.

On the occasions that I get together with my remaining family of origin, we find it a challenge to avoid pushing each other's emotional buttons. We do it

173

without thinking—it's been hard-wired into us. The triggers in my family could have armed the troops in World War II. We have our share of laughs as well. I love my sisters and nieces, and we hope, pray, and wish the best for each other.

It was during my Army stint in Korea that my talent and connection with dogs dawned crystal clear. Discovering those gifts jump-started my will to do something about my maladaptive behaviors. Healing takes time. Working through a legacy of abuse is a lifelong journey. Some issues I may never be entirely rid of, but I've stopped beating up on myself.

Who better to have helped me than dogs—those angels and best friends of humans—descendants of gray wolves (*Canis lupus*) that had packed up with humans thousands of years ago. Attracted to the outskirts of human encampments where garbage was discarded, wolves hung out waiting for scraps of food long before the existence of squeaky toys, clickers, or highly refined treats.

The wolves that were allowed to stay near humans are thought to have been relatively nonaggressive individuals that didn't threaten their hosts. Humans most likely would have killed any wolves that showed aggression.

Dogs (*Canis lupus familiaris*) were domesticated from those more approachable wolves, and they became adept at reading human emotions and behavior. The relationship between dogs and humans has grown and evolved over thousands of years to become a magnificent success for both species. We now give dogs great veterinary care and feed them consistently wonderful superfood combinations that extend their lives.

In return, dogs perform many services for us. They work with search and rescue personnel, protect livestock and property, guide the visually impaired, and help folks with disabilities manage independent lives. Therapeutic benefits provided by canines include tension relief and lowered blood pressure in stressed, anxious, or lonely individuals. With their phenomenal noses, dogs sniff out cancer, high blood sugar, epileptic seizures, drugs, and bombs that threaten our military troops, first responders, and our way of life.

I'm so grateful for the dogs I've lived and worked with. Dogs listened to me, which was a lot of what I needed. Their quiet messages via wagging tails and wiggling bodies, their imploring big eyes hanging on my every expression, their attentiveness to my many moods, their forgiving my mistakes with happy licks and playfulness—all helped wash away my ingrained self-perception as a failure.

The physicality of dogs and their innate love of walking taught me how essential movement and exercise are for depleting excess energy, anxiety, and stress, all while generating endorphins, vitality, muscle tone, and a feeling of calm. While I was rehabilitating abused and fearful rescues, they were rehabilitating *me*. They fostered within me a transformative process that moved me up a rung or two on my own evolutionary ladder. With dogs by my side, I learned to love myself.

My canine friends showered upon me all the trophies, rainbows, and unicorns a person could ever wish for. In this way they enlightened me. I ultimately understood that praise given for performing a welcome behavior was much more effective than criticism or punishment rendered for an unwelcome one.

I don't suffer fools, so I avoid them. Dogs are my bliss—they don't harbor any duplicity. They're straight with people. Over and over, they forgive and love unconditionally. They are among the most honest, loyal, and social animals on the planet.

I hope I've communicated some helpful insights and examples about how the more you walk, train, and nurture these amazing creatures, the better you'll become, not just yourself, but together as a team—you, your dog, and *your pack*.

If you prefer to be unhappy, don't get a dog and condemn it to a life of misery. But if you can be open to falling in love and accepting a dog's adoring devotion, you've got a chance! Every day we have a choice to strive for a glass-half-full or glass-half-empty outlook. I choose the former because on daily walks my dogs lift my spirits to smile, laugh, and love via furry leaps, wagging tails, and beaming smiles.

So I shower, shave, and prepare myself each day by looking in the mirror and offering myself "good boys" galore with joy in my voice. It works!

THE WOLF WHO CRIED HELP

I leave you with one last story about an unusual task on which I was sent. I will always remember the extraordinary animal I met that day.

The dispatch came through in a whispery, disembodied voice over my cell phone. My mission was to drive to one of the bleakest, most crowded dog shelters owned and operated by Maricopa County, Arizona, to evaluate a large Northern-mix canine for aggression. Was the animal worthy of further rescue efforts? Was it part wolf?

Once I'd made my assessment, I was to report back to Dr. Penny Baker, then director of Arizona Siberian Husky Rescue & Adoption, Inc. (ASHRA). She was a compassionate soul, tireless in her efforts to save animals.

Exiting the I-10 highway at Buckeye, I cruised past the desperate tent city (an extension of the Maricopa County jail from 1993–2017) operated by Sheriff Joe Arpaio, the toughest lawman in the West. I found myself awash in the despair emanating through its chain-link fencing topped with razor wire. Beyond this facility, I was greeted by another depressing county structure housing lost, abandoned, and surrendered dogs and cats awaiting disposition.

Entering the building, I informed staff that I was there to assess a dog for ASHRA and stated the run number that Penny had provided to me. A beleaguered employee led me through a maze of hallways bordered by run after run of barking dogs frantic for attention. In the cacophony, I took one step at a time and avoided eye contact with the hopeless animals flanking my path.

We reached the cell where a lanky canine with matted fur stood quiet. Somewhat shy, he backed up as I entered his pen rear-first, a less threatening position that allowed him to sniff me out. As he cautiously sidled up on my left, I slipped a choke chain over his regal head, snapped on a leash and exited to a fenced outdoor yard where I could examine his behavior far from the madding crowd.

To be less intimidating, I squatted while soothing him with praise. He responded by lying down, rolling over, and exposing his belly and throat, which I stroked gently. His wolf-like submission touched my heart.

Despite his unkempt, malnourished condition, he was magnificent. This "beast" had a coat of black and silver sable that one could easily imagine would be drop-dead gorgeous after a proper bath and brushing. His golden eyes bored into my soul, begging for help to escape the fetid limbo.

Returning to his run, we walked the gauntlet of raucous animals clamoring at their gates in a last-ditch effort for liberation. The rattling gates held. When I shut the hybrid back in his spot, I reassured him that someone would soon be back for him.

During his intake to the shelter, the possibility of wolf being part of his make-up had been raised as an issue. Public shelters are bound by law to euthanize a wolf or even a dog that is part wolf. If I officially identified the fellow as part wolf, I would sign his death warrant.

I made my way to the office and informed the staff that the dog was a husky-malamute mix and not part wolf as had been suspected. They beamed at the good news, always welcome in that house of blues. I'm not usually one to fib, but to save an innocent life? *You betcha.*

Driving away from the shelter, I phoned Dr. Baker and told her that our charge was indeed a wolf mix (also known as a wolf dog) but not aggressive. How much wolf he possessed I didn't know, but because he had a mild beta temperament (not typically the case with wolf mixes, so you must be careful around them), I was confident that she could place a slip collar over his head, attach a leash to him, and lead him away. I said she could place him in her back seat and drive him to freedom.

Relief sounded in her voice as she informed me of a wolf sanctuary in Tonopah—just fifty miles west of Phoenix—that rescued abandoned wolves and wolf dogs. They had several wolf packs on forty acres. She was going to contact them and hoped they would take him in. Now she could get started on the paperwork for the dog's release.

My spirit thrilled at the possibility. That splendid animal could soon join his own kind in a protected area where he could pack up and live a fulfilling life after teetering on the brink of euthanasia. To this day, I can close my eyes, see his beauty, and conjure his unspoken thoughts cutting into my core: Please, sir, help me get out of here.

Fast-forward to when Dr. Baker arrived at the wolf sanctuary with the hybrid. They asked her how she had transported him—was he crated? She replied, "He's curled up in my back seat," and explained that her trainer had assured her the canine was submissive.

Thanks to Dr. Baker, I'd been part of a mission of mercy that allowed me to right several wrongs by using my expertise. I'm also thankful for ASHRA volunteers like Ann Colano, and unsung others, for inviting me to participate in such redemptive enterprises.

When I caught up with Dr. Baker much later, she informed me that the sanctuary owners made the wolf dog the "house wolf." He lived inside with them, bringing them much joy and love.

Eventually, DNA analysis indicated that he was greater than 80 percent wolf. How is this possible? The offspring (wolf dogs) produced by a wolf and a dog are *not* sterile. Wolves and dogs are very closely related genetically. Dogs are a subspecies of wolf (*Canis lupus*) — the full scientific name for dogs is *Canis lupus familiaris* (often seen shortened to *Canis familiaris*). Hence, if a wolf dog or its progeny mate with a pure wolf or another wolf dog, the pups of those resulting litters could contain more than 50 percent wolf DNA.

The emotions I felt in the presence of that majestic wolf dog overwhelmed me. I rededicated myself to being the best trainer I could be, and I will train the descendants of wolves for as long as I can. When I die, I would love to come back as a wolf. May their great spirits forever run free.

Before You Go

Thank you so much for reading my story. If you enjoyed this book, my pack and I would be grateful if you would please rate *The Power of the Pack* online wherever you bought this book—and if you would like to add a few words in a review, that would be great too! You may keep it brief or simply give it a rating using the stars.

Your helpful reviews are also welcome on Goodreads, BookBub, BookPage, and other review sites you visit. Active on social media? If you please, mention *The Power of the Pack* and its positive message to your friends and followers. Heartfelt thanks to you for your support.

Acknowledgments

My sincere thanks to: C. Russell (compilation and edits); Kelsey Harding (cover design); I. Litscher (tech assistance); Beta readers Anne A., Les Dickey, MB Fisher, Ashlyn Harding, P. Helmetag, E. and J. Karstens, and D. Robinson; and L. Gorman.

I thank all my 110th MP Company sentry platoon compatriots, especially Phil Nissan and Richard Conklin, for having my back.

Kudos to the Arizona Siberian Husky Rescue & Adoption, Inc. (ASHRA), Dr. Penny Baker, Ann Colano, Healing Hearts Rescue of Phoenix, Litter League Rescue of Phoenix, and many unsung volunteers—it warms my heart to engage with humans who do unto others with purely altruistic motives.

I'm grateful to Suzanne Shelden of Shelden Studios and Sandra Olivetti Martin, publisher of New Bay Books, for bringing this book to publication.

Thanks also to my higher power, wherever She is.

I owe special thanks and appreciation to the love of my life Lana Carson.

PHOTO CREDITS

BEAR SETS THE HOOK
Bear
P. H. Russell Jr.

Sentry dog (foreground) riveted on a "perp" in a padded suit
US Army, Camp Ames Yearbook, 1969. Accessed via chitgussin, "Camp Ames Korea US Army 1969 Video Year Book Part 2 – 110th Military Police Company," compilation including multiple years, YouTube video (screen shot at 5:36), May 3, 2013, https://www.youtube.com/watch?v=2-iDYhdldc8.

The author on the right, straddling Bear
P. H. Russell Jr.

MP watch tower
US Army, Camp Ames Yearbook, 1972. Accessed via chitgussin, "Camp Ames," 4:48.

MP watch towers along the inner and outer barbed wire perimeters, Camp Ames, South Korea
US Army, Camp Ames Yearbook, 1972. Accessed via chitgussin, "Camp Ames," 4:41.

DUKE
The author and Duke, circa 1954
P. H. Russell Jr.

BAD DOGS WITH MIDNIGHT AND AIKO
Midnight
P. H. Russell Jr.

Aiko
P. H. Russell Jr.

STRYDER THE LAB-RABBIT
Stryder
P. H. Russell Jr.

A FEAR-BOUND AUSTRALIAN SHEPHERD
Romeo Jr. (RJ)
P. H. Russell Jr.

Juliet, Lana, and RJ
P. H. Russell Jr.

About the Author

With over thirty-five years of experience boarding dogs and training dogs in obedience, tracking, and security, Pierce H. Russell Jr. has learned much about man's best friend and how the power of the pack can foster harmony, good behavior, and mutual positive bonding.

Raised in upstate New York, Pierce discovered his passion for training while serving as a US Army sentry dog handler in South Korea during the Vietnam War. Having grown up in a dysfunctional family environment, he found purpose, love, and redemption while working and living with canines. Pierce now resides in Phoenix, Arizona, with his beloved pack.